INTRODUCTION

*8 top left
This large wall-painting of the Buddha Attisha is typical of Tibet's religious traditions.*

8 top right As this photograph of the Yorlung river near Samye shows, the Tibet landscape is generally bare with small cultivated areas close to the villages.

8-9 Some of Asia's largest rivers have their sources in Tibet. The most important is the Tsang-po.

9 top Yumbulagang Palace (ca. A.D.600) was the first masonry residence to be built for the rulers of the Yarlung Dynasty.

9 bottom Throughout central Tibet the villages still maintain the features of traditional Tibetan architecture.

Tibet has been given many names but the "Heart of Asia" seems the most appropriate. This vast plateau, almost as large as Europe, that both separates and joins the Mongolian steppes to the Indian plains is, and has always been, an immense crossroads of races, cultures, ethnic groups, religions, and civilizations. Perhaps no other place in Asia has captured the imagination and unconscious awareness of the West as much as Tibet; Europeans have liked to consider the country as the mystical receptacle of all the hopes, fantasies, dreams, and desires that the West does not (or did not) succeed in fulfilling. It was thought of as the Shangri-La of the spirit, a mythical country where wise men could fly, the people were happy, and some had even discovered the secret of immortality. That was how Tibet was described in certain travel accounts of the nineteenth and early twentieth centuries. Obviously, that was never the case. Like other countries on earth, Tibet has never been a terrestrial paradise, the people have never

all been completely happy, and no one has discovered the elixir of life. However, Tibetan civilization is one of great importance. Though little developed in terms of material progress, it had made enormous strides with regard to philosophy and spirituality. Whichever social group they belonged to, the people demonstrated a cultural cohesion that could not be rivaled by the surrounding Asian countries. Fewer than six million people lived in an immense area shared by nomads, shepherds, farmers, and the inhabitants of the few small towns. The monks, who, in the mid-twentieth century, represented over ten percent of the entire population, were a group apart. Lhasa, the capital and center of the Roof of the World, was the home of the Dalai Lama, who presided over a government composed of both lay and religious members and whose authority was accepted throughout all the country. Profoundly imbued by the spirituality of Buddhism and Bon (the autochthonous religion), Tibetan civilization, though not the paradise imagined in the West, was able to offer its men and women a serene and stimulating existence.

Italy has always had a special relationship with Tibet and, thanks to Italian missionaries, travelers, and orientalists, has provided an important contribution to the knowledge and study of the country, its cultures, and religions. Even though Odorico da

Pordenone and Marco Polo never visited Tibet, they were the first to speak of it in their travel accounts. In the eighteenth century, Capuchin and Jesuit missionaries succeeded in entering Tibet and remaining there for several decades. At the beginning of the eighteenth century, the Capuchins even opened a mission in Lhasa, which operated for over fifty years. The Jesuit father Ippolito Desideri was the first expert on Tibet, having lived in Lhasa from March 1716 until April 1721. Desideri had arrived in the city after a long and adventurous journey across Kashmir, Ladak, and all of western Tibet, during which he visited Mount Kailash and Lake Manasarovar. During his stay, the Tuscan Jesuit, who was born on December 20, 1684 in Pistoia to a family of aristocratic origin, studied the principal Buddhist texts. Another Italian Catholic missionary, Orazio della Penna, wrote the first known Tibetan dictionary. It seems that, after passing through several hands, the manuscript was found in the possession of a certain Schroter, who translated it from Italian to English and published it in Serampore in 1826. More recently, the Italian orientalist Giuseppe Tucci (1894-1985) contributed greatly to the knowledge of Tibet as a result of his several stays there. Between 1928 and 1948, Tucci organized eight expeditions to various areas of the Land of the Snows, unveiling many of the mysteries of the culture of that almost unknown land to the Western mind. In particular, his survey of all the works of art in western and central Tibet still represents a study of enormous value in the field of Tibetology. After Tucci, Tibet was visited by the Italian author Fosco Maraini (in 1937 and 1948), who published perhaps the last great portrayal of the Tibetan world before the Chinese invasion titled *Segreto Tibet*, which met with enormous critical and public acclaim.

Sadly, threatening clouds began to build up over the Land of the Snows during the second half of the 1940's, culminating in a storm of unheard of violence in 1950 when the troops of the People's Republic of China invaded and occupied Tibet. Until that

12 top left Women have always played a role of great importance and dignity in Tibetan society and have never experienced the subjugation to which women in other traditional Asiatic societies have been exposed.

12 bottom left Tibetans can divorce, men can remarry widows, and women, particularly in nomadic communities, can enjoy polyandric marriages, i.e. have more than one husband.

12 right Sometimes Tibetan children still wear traditional clothes.

13 top left and right Men of all ages in Tibet often wear coral earrings. Their long hair is tied back and adorned with ivory and turquoise rings.

13 bottom It is very uncommon for the face of Tibetans, whichever ethnic group they belong to, not to split open into a broad smile.

time it had been a sovereign state and quite different to China in terms of ethnic groups, social system, culture, religion, and traditions. There is no denying that the events following the invasion reduced the vast cultural and artistic patrimony of Tibet to a disturbing degree, but fortunately, since the early 1980's, positive changes have taken place in China's attitude and monasteries have been rebuilt or restored, the main festivities reintroduced, and a certain freedom of religion permitted. Although the wounds caused by its recent terrible past are still visible, in some ways the Roof of the World has started once more to flourish. Even in the midst of a difficult situation, it is now possible to come across important fragments of the ancient civilization that belongs not just to the inhabitants of Tibet but to all of humanity. The existence of these fragments obliges us to place the optimism of will above the pessimism of reason. Above all, it obliges us to believe that Tibet will succeed in demonstrating that when a tradition has deep and solid roots, it will prevail over even the most difficult trials and emerge triumphant.

16-17 One of the loveliest sights in the mountain passes in Tibet are the "Lung-ta," the multicolored flags on which prayers or sacred symbols are printed whose blessings are dispersed through the air by the energy of the wind.

18-19 At dawn the purity of the Himalayan light clearly reveals the peaks of Everest.

Mount Muztagh
(25,354 ft) ▲

Kunlun mountains

Ghang Tang

Gomo •

Tibetan Plateau

• Gêrzê

• Lhazhong

Mount Kailash
(22,027 ft)
▲

La'nga
Co

Lake
Manasarovar

Purang

H

i

m

N

e

p

a

l

India

a

l

Saga
•

Yarlung Tsangpo

Lhatse
•
• Shigatse •

• Tingri

Kathmandu •

Mount Everest
(29,029 ft) ▲

China

Tsinghai

Tangula Shan

Amdo

Baqên

Biru

Nam Co

Chamdo

Banbar Lhorong

Bomi

Lhasa

Baxoi

antse

Yarlung Tsangpo

a

s

Ningxia

India

a

y

Bhutan Cona

Myanmar

The origins of the Tibetan people are still somewhat mysterious. Local tradition recounts that the original ancestors of the inhabitants of the Land of the Snows were large monkeys – the incarnation of the goddess Chenrezig – and a sort of female ogre that was worshiped as a guardian spirit of the mountains.

Mythology aside, modern anthropology places the Tibetans among the huge ethnic group known as Mongols, including various peoples of central Asia. The inhabitants of the central regions of U and Tsang, and in large part also those in western Tibet, are of medium height, have a round head, and pronounced cheekbones. Those that live in the eastern and northern provinces of Kham and Amdo are tall, have elongated heads, and long arms and legs. They all have straight black hair and dark, almond-shaped eyes.

Unlike their physical characteristics, their linguistic grouping is unrelated to the world of the Mongols. Whereas the Tibetan language shares several points in common with certain dialects of the Himalayas, it has more in common with the language of Myanmar, to the extent that experts speak of "Tibeto-Burmese." Like their ethnic background, the origins of Tibetan history are also little known today. Local tradition speaks of a mythic age in which a dynasty of celestial kings governed. They were gods who descended to Earth to rule, though they lived in heaven. According to Tibetan chronicles, it was the custom for these kings to rule until their eldest son learned to ride (something that generally happened around the age of thirteen), which coincided with their coming of age. This attainment of adulthood marked the shift of regal power, and the old king would die in the sense that he would return permanently to heaven by means of a magic cord, often associated with rainbows. The first of these heavenly kings, Nyatri Tsempo, descended to Earth in the valley of the river Yarlung in central

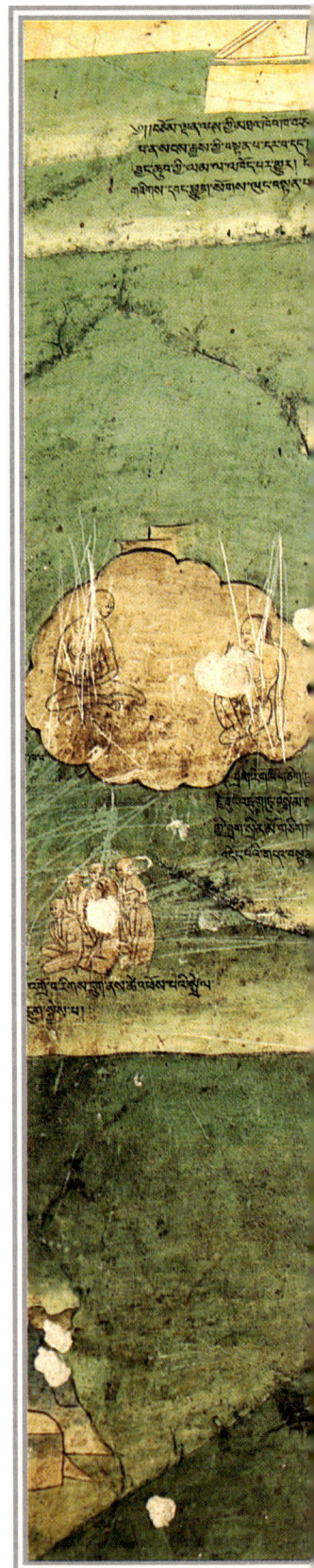

20 According to tradition, Nyatri Tsenpo, portrayed in this tanka *(a painting on fabric) in the Museum Guimet in Paris, was the ruler who founded the Yarlung Dynasty after descending from heaven to earth.*

20-21 Faithful to legend, a fresco in Samye Monastery illustrates the origin of the Tibetan people from the union of a monkey (the incarnation of the divinity Chenrezig) with a female ogre.

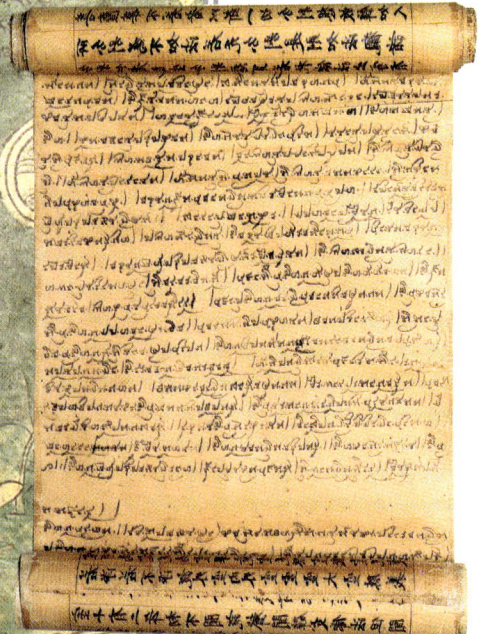

Tibet and settled his dynasty there. It seems that before his arrival Tibetans did not live in brick or stone buildings but in caves or natural shelters. Nyatri Tsempo moved the Tibetan people decisively along the road of development by building a small but imposing castle (the one still known today as Yumbulagang) on a hill. The king and his first six successors did not leave human remains when they returned to heaven on their magic cord, therefore was no need to build them funerary monuments. It was only from the time of the eighth king, Drigum Tsempo, that the magic cord was cut and their bodies, being unable to return to heaven, required a tomb. The funerary monument of Drigum Tsempo, which the Tibetans still call "the first tomb of the kings," proves that this king really existed and testifies to important events of the country, thus confirming a sort of prehistory in which certain elements can be verified and dated, thereby emerging from the mists of legend.

Events in the Land of the Snows enter a historical dimension around the seventh century A.D. when the society was feudal, strongly hierarchical, and led by Songtsen Gampo (known also as Tride Songtsen), the thirty-second king of Yarlung. Songtsen Gampo succeeded in the arduous task of uniting the different tribes of north-central Asia, which were all fundamentally part of the Tibetan ethnic group, under a single command.

At the time of this ruler, much of

modern central Tibet was unified and its inhabitants were able to carry out daring and successful military raids on what is today Chinese territory.

As the only sizeable urban center during the reign of Songtsen Gampo, Lhasa became the capital of the country, and thanks to military expeditions to the north and west, large portions of neighboring territories were annexed.

Until the reign of Songtsen Gampo, the religion of the Tibetan people had been Bon (sometimes written Pon), though the nature of the cult and its spiritual elements are still unknown to scholars. Hypotheses mostly agree that Bon was based on nature, a sort of magical animism that centered on the figure of a priest whose task was to perform divinatory practices and rituals.

22 left Tenpa Sherab was the founder of the Bon religion, the spiritual path followed by Tibetans before the arrival of Buddhism.

22 right The monarchs of the ancient Yarlung Dynasty, like Songtsen Gampo, the first Buddhist

king, are still worshiped in a manner similar to that reserved for the lamas and spiritual masters of the past.

In 635, Songtsen Gampo married the Nepalese princess Bhrikuti Devi (Belsa in Tibetan), and in 641, Wen-c'eng Kung-chu (Gyasa in Tibetan), who was the daughter of the Chinese emperor T'ai Tsung. Tradition has it that these two women brought many gifts, including Buddhist writings and images (Buddhism was already widespread in both China and Nepal), constituting the first appearances of the new religion in Tibet. The most important gift was undoubtedly Gyasa's statue of Buddha Sakyamuni that, allegedly, had been blessed by the Buddha himself. This statue still exists in the Jokhang Temple where it is visited by an unending stream of pilgrims. However, even though it was practiced by the two princesses, Buddhism did not elicit much interest among the people in the seventh century, who considered it a foreign concept. Songtsen Gampo, on the other hand, was curious, and he ordered a writing system to be created for the Tibetan language (as until that time it was only spoken) so that the Buddhist texts could be translated into Tibetan. He invited a number of learned men to travel to Tibet from India to study the Tibetan language in order to invent a proper alphabet and so that the Land of the Snows, like all the surrounding countries, could translate its phonetic sounds into signs. The scholar entrusted with the task, Thonmi Sambota, returned to Tibet a few years later with an alphabet derived from the Brahmin and Gupta scripts, which were similar to Sanskrit and very common at that time in the kingdoms of north-central India and the Himalayas. The adoption of an alphabet that was Indian in derivation emphasizes the cultural link that connected Tibet with India, despite the ethnic differences of their peoples, and which was further strengthened over the centuries with the spread of Buddhism into Tibet. As many writers have noted, the espousal of a particular form of writing is a cultural decision with deep implications that go beyond the merely technical matter of written communication. The creation of an alphabet similar to Sanskrit meant that, a thousand years or so ago, as Tibet entered fully into the cultural world of India it moved irreversibly away from that of China.

Following Songtsen Gampo's death in 649, his successors further enlarged the boundaries of his kingdom turning Tibet into one of the most powerful and feared kingdoms in Central Asia. In 755, the throne was inherited by Trisong Deutsen, who became the most important of all the rulers of the Yarlung Dynasty. Trisong Deutsen organized brief but successful military expeditions that struck at the heart of the Chinese empire and forced the emperor of the Middle Kingdom to sign a humiliating peace treaty. Yet, the true importance of this king lies in the fact that he built the foundations for the introduction of Buddhism into Tibet when he invited two great Indian Buddhist masters,

Santarakshita and Padmasambhava, to the Land of the Snows. The former was a man of great learning at the university in Nalanda who established the monastic system in Tibet, while the extraordinary personal charisma of the latter helped him to overcome the great resistance to the new faith put up by the followers of Bon. During Trisong Deutsen's reign, the first Buddhist monastery, Samye, was built, and in the confrontation between the Indian and Chinese schools of Buddhism, it was the first that held sway. Trisong Deutsen died in 797 but his policies were perpetuated, though less effectively, by two of his four sons: Muni Tsenpo and Tride Songtsen. In 815, Tride Songtsen's third son, Ralpachen,

generally considered the third great ruler of the Yarlung Dynasty, took the throne. He finally put an end to the war with China and signed a treaty in which relations between the two countries were normalized. Unfortunately for Ralpachen, his sympathy for the Buddhist religion as opposed to that of Bon aroused envy, jealousy, and resentment among his court. A group of Bon supporters took advantage of the situation and organized a bloody palace conspiracy. They appealed to the chauvinist feelings of certain aristocratic families who still considered Buddhism foreign to Tibet and they honed the fears of the Bon priests by claiming that their ancient religion would be completely supplanted by the new one.

Alleging that foreigners were manipulating the king, the conspirators hatched a plot that culminated in 838 with the assassination of Ralpachen and the succession of his elder brother Langdarma. Langdarma was a bitter opponent of Buddhism and cracked down on the religion so hard that he is still remembered today. The temples and monasteries were closed and profaned, the monks killed or forced into abjuration, and all public or external manifestations of Buddhism were banned. Langdarma's persecution of the religion was so extreme that a monk called Lhalungpa Pelgy Dorje decided to break his vow of non-violence and kill the king. The story recounts that the monk disguised himself as a Bon-po priest, entered the royal palace during a festivity, and managed to shoot the king with an arrow from a bow he had hidden in the sleeves of his outer tunic.

The death of the bloodthirsty king brought both the Yarlung Dynasty and the political unity of Tibet to a close. Having been one of Asia's strongest empires for four hundred years, for the next few centuries Tibet was split in a large number of tiny princedoms that were often at war with one another. The memory of the past greatness of Tibet remained only in the western area of the country where a branch of the Yarlung Dynasty created the kingdoms of Guge and Purang. These two played a major role in the cultural history of the Himalayan region by developing an artistic and religious tradition of a very high level. On the other hand, the central and eastern provinces of the former Tibet entered a period of political confusion in which the effects of the absence of an authoritative power were strongly detrimental.

24-25 Some of the wall frescoes in Samye Monastery date to its foundation in the eighth century.

25 bottom left The meeting of the king Trison Deutsen and the great yogi Padmasambhava is a favorite theme of Tibetan paintings.

25 right Padmasambhava was the Tantric master who brought Buddhism to Tibet in the eighth century. He is worshiped by Tibetans as a "second Buddha."

26 Sakya, founded by Khon Konchog Gyalpo, is one of Tibetan Buddhism's most important schools, and its lamas are easily recognizable by the unusual shape of their ceremonial hats.

27 Another important figure from the school founded by Khon Konchog Gyalpo is Kunga Gyaltsen, who is seen in this tanka in Sakya debating with Indian and Tibetan Buddhist masters.

Having forgotten its imperial past, in the late tenth and early eleventh centuries Tibet experienced a renewed interest in Buddhism. The spirituality of the Roof of the World and India was revitalized and an open flow of contacts between the countries ensued. Indian religious masters went to teach in Tibet and Tibetan scholars traveled to the main Buddhist universities in India to deepen their knowledge. Around the year 1000, a second expansion of the Buddhist doctrine led to the religion supplanting the importance of Bon in Tibet and to the development of four principal Buddhist schools, those of Nyingma, Sakya, Kagyu, and Kadam-Gelug. Many important monasteries (*gompa* in Tibetan) were built during the next two hundred years, such as Tshurpu, Sakya, Drigung, Talung, Reting, and many others which quickly assumed such importance that they took on a social as well as religious significance. The wide diffusion of Buddhism had created in Tibet a general cultural environment that the great majority of the population accepted, but from a political standpoint the country remained fragmented.

In the eleventh and twelfth centuries the various kings, princes, and feudal lords that governed the region managed to live together without ex-

28 The founder of the Mongol empire, Genghis Khan, was elected king in 1196. The Mongols, who were converted to Buddhism by Tibetan lamas, played a major role at certain periods in Tibetan political history.

cessive tension and this period is remembered as being peaceful. However, this interlude ended at the start of the thirteenth century when the Mongol tribes to the north, in an immense area that covered almost all of Central Asia, began to migrate. Under the guidance of intelligent, determined leaders, these proud, warlike, and aggressive peoples began to dominate nations and peoples. Even China, the proud Middle Kingdom, fell to their

assault. In 1207, Genghis Khan, the supreme Mongol leader, sent his emissaries to Tibet to request the region's submission, to which there was no alternative as the Tibetans knew there was no way they could possibly oppose the powerful Mongol forces. In 1239, the cavalry vanguard led by Godan, the grandson of Genghis Khan, entered deep into the country and reached the central provinces of U and Tsang. The fate of Tibet seemed already decided when an unforeseeable event occurred: made curious by the reports from his men of the great influence exerted in Tibet by yogis and lamas, Godan invited the most distinguished spiritual master of the age, Sakya Pandita, the head of the Sakya Buddhist school, to his court. The relationship that developed between the Mongol chief and Buddhist master was complex and profound; owing to his exceptional personal charisma, the lama succeeded in converting Godan to Buddhism, who, as a sign of devo-

tion, not only forbade further incursion into Tibet but made the abbots of the Sakya school the governors of the entire country. This relationship, often described by historians as lama-patron, resulted in Tibet being governed by Tibetans (the Sakya abbots) but under the direct protection of the Mongol *khan*, who wished to make manifest and solidify his spiritual link with the Land of the Snows and its religion by providing his personal support. The lama-patron relationship between Godan Khan and Sakya Pandita was continued under their successors: Kublai Khan, Godan's son, was so fascinated by the personality and spirituality of Phagpa, Sakya Pandita's grandson, that he conferred upon him the title of Imperial Tutor, which was the equivalent of "Ruler of Tibet." The Sakya hierarchy governed Tibet

29 left Frescoes in temples often show the most important lamas from the school of Buddhism to which the monastery belongs. These are two abbots from the Sakyapa order.

29 right Lama Sakya Pandita converted the Mongol khan, Godan, to Buddhism, thereby saving Tibet from invasion by this people of the north.

for almost one hundred years, but when the power of the Mongol Yuan Dynasty in China began to wane, the power of Sakya was weakened.

In the Yarlung valley, the powerful Pamotrupa family placed itself at the head of a strong nationalist movement that openly contested the abbots of Sakya, and the power of the monastery came to a complete end in 1354. Jangchub Gyaltsen, the strong man of the Pamotrupa clan, formed a new government that was recognized by the *khans* as an indication of the end of their rule in China. When the Ming Dynasty replaced the Yuan at the helm of the Middle

monks or lamas, the dynasty was strongly secular but allowed the various Buddhist schools and reborn Bon religion to exist freely and in mutual harmony. The most important religious authorities in Tibet continued to be held in the highest esteem but their authority was now purely spiritual and not political. The abbots of the largest monasteries continued to exercise such a powerful social influence, especially at a local level, that they took advantage of by forming alliances with this or that governor, but the overall authority in the country was nonetheless held by lay hands. The fall of the Pamotrupa Dynasty in 1435 brought to an end a period that had been positive for Tibetan history but that was followed by two centuries of strife in which rival factions pulled apart a divided Tibet.

The 130-year rule of the princes of Rinpung was as secular as the Pamotrupa's had been. It lasted until 1565 when power passed to the kings of Tsang, which became the third of the great dynasties to rule over Tibet between the fifteenth and seventeenth centuries. Each had exercised its authority in complete independence without ever making a gesture, even formal, of subjection to the emperors of China.

Kingdom, Jangchub Gyaltsen decided that the lama-patron relationship was a thing of the past and so the link between Tibet and a foreign power came to an end. At this stage, Tibet was able to consider itself to all effects independent once again.

The period of the Pamotrupa Dynasty coincided with the rise of a widespread sense of identity that was most broadly expressed in the re-evaluation of the role of the ancient Yarlung kings. Songtsen Gampo and Trisong Deutsen were made the objects of veneration that was almost religious in nature. Although some of the Pamotrupa governors were

31 bottom These stuccoes portray the most highly venerated Tibetan kings: Songtsen Gampo, Trisong Deutsen, and Ralpachen. They made the greatest efforts to spread Buddhism in Tibet.

32 top This tanka shows the most important masters of the Sakya school. Every Buddhist school in Tibet has a sacred genealogical tree that outlines the spiritual lineage of its masters.

32 bottom This eighteenth-century statue shows a lama from the Gelug tradition. Each Tibetan school is distinguished by the ceremonial hat worn by its adepts.

At the start of the 1400's, the influence of the lamas began to increase in one of the most important lines of reincarnation in the Gelug Buddhist school. Sonam Gyatso, the third of these incarnations, established a strong relationship with several Mongol tribes which – though they no longer governed China – were still a notable political and military power in Central Asia. Altan Khan, a descendant of Genghis, became a disciple of Sonam Gyatso and, as a mark of devotion, conferred the title of Dalai Lama on his master, which, from that moment on, has distinguished all successive incarnations of this master. Before long, the figure of the Dalai Lama acquired a strong social, as well as religious, profile in Tibet, particularly in the central and western areas. The fifth Dalai Lama, Ngawang Lobsang Gyatso, was a man of great political skills and strong personality. He was extremely sensitive to the divisions created in his country by the internal power struggles between clans, princedoms, and even the large monasteries. The first decades of the seventeenth century were dramatic for Tibet. The power of the kings of Tsang had weakened but no one capable to rivaling them had emerged. In this context, the fifth Dalai Lama, having placed himself at the head of a broad front of opponents, succeeded in making himself the only effective challenger to the kings of Tsang, and after a bitter struggle of varying fortunes, the Tsang were defeated in 1642.

The victory of the Dalai Lama and his allies was made possible by, most importantly, the alliance that Ngawang Lobsang Gyatso had formed with Gushri Khan, head of the powerful Qosot tribe of Mongols. The support of the Mongol troops proved decisive, and from the mid-seventeenth century on, Tibet was pacified, united, and independent under the fifth Dalai Lama.

The nation had finally found a point of reference, both spiritual and political. From this time on, the reincarnated Dalai Lama ceased to be simply one of the main lineages of the Gelug school of Buddhism and became the symbol of Tibet and all its inhabitants, regardless of ethnic grouping, social position, or religious faith.

33 left This is a detail of the famous gold seal of the fifth Dalai Lama, struck in 1652.

33 right Some Buddhist teachings, like these works from the sixteenth to eighteenth centuries, contain illustrations that make them genuine works of art.

34 left The hand prints of the fifth Dalai Lama are found on an edict asking the Tibetan people to obey the regent Sangye Gyatso.

34 right The government of the fifth Dalai Lama reunified Tibet, which, for the first time since the Yarlung Dynasty, once again played a

major role in Asian politics. As this painting from Samye shows, a great many ambassadors paid homage to the Dalai Lama.

35 Desi Sangye Gyatso, the fifth Dalai Lama's regent, was much venerated by Tibetans. This tanka shows him in a position of honor above the protector Shanlon.

The years under the fifth Dalai Lama passed into history as synonymous with good government and national stability, but problems arose as soon as the "Precious Protector" died in 1682. His most important collaborator, Desi Sangye Gyatso, did not reveal the death of the Dalai Lama for several years, claiming that the "Presence" had retired for a period of meditation and that he would not be taking part in public ceremonies. In the end, Desi Sangye Gyatso was forced to admit the truth and offered the excuse that he had been afraid that, had the Dalai Lama's death been made public, the building of the Potala Palace would not have been finished. Construction of the Potala had been the fifth Dalai Lama's greatest wish. This excuse is not convincing but historians are unable to agree on the man's true motives. Some claim that he had been worried that a power vacuum would have resulted in a period of fratricidal conflicts, thereby undoing all the good work the fifth Dalai Lama had achieved. Others, less benign, suggest that Sangye Gyatso's behavior was dictated purely by personal greed and by the fear of being forced out of the highest levels of government. The disappointment of the Tibetans was, however, immediately compensated for by the announcement that the new incarnation of the "Precious Protector" had been found and was on his way to Lhasa to take his place in the now completed Potala.

DWELLING OF TESSALING LAMA, SHIGATZI.

MAUSOLEUM AT TESHOO LOOMBOO.

MONGOL NOBLE.

LEH, LITTLE THIBET.

CHINESE WALL.

SCALE
50 100 200 300 Miles

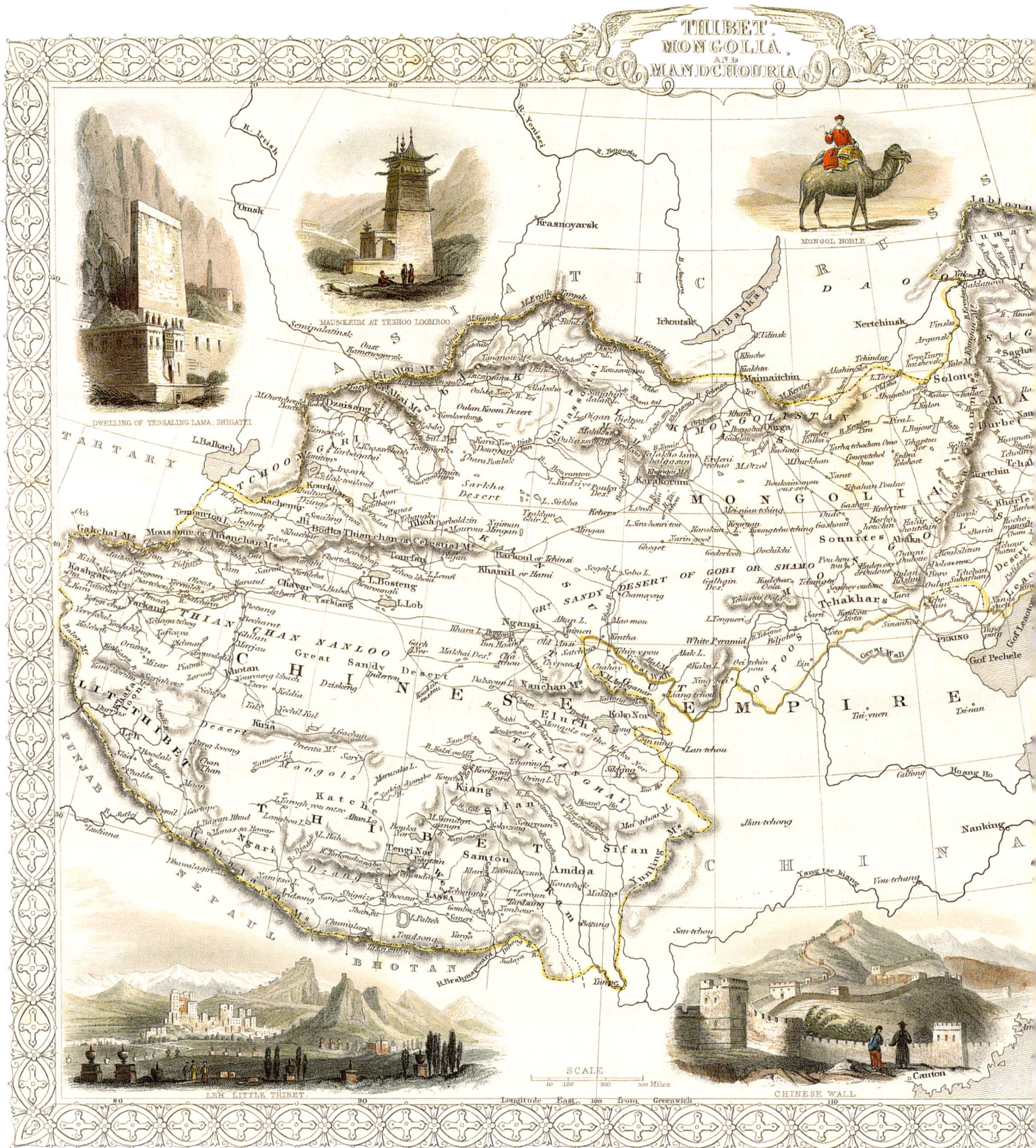

The sixth Dalai Lama was an eccentric person and, unfortunately, his unusual behavior was used as a pretext by foreign powers to intervene in the internal affairs of Tibet. Not wishing to expose himself in person, the Chinese emperor, Ch'ing (Manchu Dynasty), encouraged a cruel and unscrupulous Mongol chief called Lhazang Khan to enter Tibet. The legitimate government in Lhasa was deposed with the accusation that it was not able to control the young, wayward Gyalwa Rinpoche, and also that it was heavily influenced by men who had worked with the previous Dalai Lama. In particular, Desi Sangye Gyatso was killed, all his ministers imprisoned, and the sixth Dalai Lama was placed under house arrest. Lhazang Khan offered Tibet as a gift to the Manchu emperor who returned the favor by appointing the Mongol as its governor.

After his capture, the sixth Dalai Lama was invited to China but he died during the journey under myste-

36-37 This 1851 print depicts Central Asia. The drawings below show, from left to right, the royal palace in Leh (Ladak), the Great Wall of China (near Canton), and the Potala (Lhasa).

37 bottom Kang Hsi was the Manchu emperor who sent an army to Tibet to defeat the Zungari Mongols.

FORTRESS AND PALACE OF DALAI LAMA, LASSA.

previously established an alliance with Desi Sangye Gyatso. Taking advantage of the resentment of the Tibetans towards Lhazang Khan – who had, among other things, tried to install his protégé as the "true" sixth Dalai Lama – the Zungari invaded Tibet in 1717, conquered Lhasa, and killed Lhazang Khan. However pleased the Tibetans were to see Lhazang dead, they soon changed their minds as the new arrivals turned out to be even worse.

Exhilarated by victory, they burned the monasteries, raped the women, and killed the men. Everything that the fifth Dalai Lama had created was washed away by the destructive wave of the Zungari.

The only person to benefit from the situation was Kang Hsi, the new Manchu emperor, who sent an army to Tibet to fight the Zungari and to escort Kalsang Gyatso, the seventh Dalai Lama, to Lhasa from Kumbun Monastery where he lived in the northeast of Amdo. The Chinese army was welcomed with joy in the Land of the Snows because it represented an end to the bloody rule of the Zungari, and because it would make the return of the Dalai Lama possible. Nonetheless, the Tibetans were forced once again to realize that in politics there is never a disinterested party. In 1720, the seventh incarnation of the "Presence" took the Lion Throne, but, in exchange, the Chinese emperor demanded that Ti-

bet be a sort of Manchu protectorate. His representatives, the Amban, settled in Lhasa accompanied by a Han garrison of 2,000 men. It was the task of the Amban to look after the interests of Beijing in Tibet.

The seventh and eighth Dalai Lamas did not exercise a very important political role, preferring to devote themselves to spiritual matters, and the affairs of state were entrusted to the Kashag, a government Cabinet, composed of four kalon (ministers) of whom three were lay and one a monk. This legislative body remained in power relatively unaltered until 1959.

rious circumstances. The death of the Dalai Lama and the brutal rule of the Mongol chief wounded the Tibetan people deeply; acts of violence and atrocities of all kinds were committed throughout the country and, even worse, Lhazang Khan's invasion whetted the appetite of another Mongol tribe, the Zungari, who had

From a political viewpoint, the eighteenth century was a dark one for Tibet. The ninth to twelfth Dalai Lamas all died young, probably poisoned in palace plots, and it was only the weakness of the Manchu empire that prevented the Land of the Snows from being completely absorbed by China. However, things changed completely in 1876, the Year of Fire, when Thubten Gyatso, the thirteenth Dalai Lama, was born.

Unlike his predecessors, Thubten Gyatso not only lived long but also governed Tibet with such intelligence and farsightedness that he was called the "Great Thirteenth." When, in 1911, the Manchu empire collapsed in Beijing and the republic was proclaimed, the thirteenth Dalai Lama reacted by declaring the complete and total independence of Tibet, and in 1914, this was sanctioned in a treaty signed by the British and Tibetan governments.

On the thirteenth day of the tenth month of the Year of the Waterbird (December 17, 1933), Thubten Gyatso died following a sudden attack of pneumonia and was replaced, on February 22, 1940, by the fourteenth Dalai Lama, Tenzin Gyatso, who had been born on July 6, 1935 in Takster, a desolate village in Amdo.

It was the task of Tenzin Gyatso to govern Tibet during the most dramatic period of its history, for on October 7, 1950 the troops of the newly created People's Republic of China crossed the Tibetan border in six places, easily overcoming the weak resistance posed by the Tibetan army.

In April 1951 a delegation of the Dalai Lama in Beijing was obliged to sign the "17-Point Declaration" in which Tibet became part of China – though under conditions of extensive autonomy – and the Chinese army entered Lhasa in September 1951, thereby finalizing the occupation of Tibet. Unfortunately the autonomy referred to in the declaration was

nothing more than words on paper, and the Chinese colonization was so brutal that it aroused a heroic though useless and bloody resistance, crushed in March 1959.

The Dalai Lama was forced to flee to India (where he still resides as a guest of the Indian government) so that he would not be deported to Beijing. Over one hundred thousand Tibetans followed him into exile where they still live as refugees in India, Nepal, Bhutan, or other countries.

In 1965, Tibet was divided up and only the central region of U-Tsang was recognized with the status of "Autonomous Region"; Amdo and Kham were incorporated into the adjacent provinces of China. The Dalai Lama, who was awarded the Nobel Peace Prize in 1989, continues his struggle for the independence of Tibet, attempting in every possible way to open a dialog with Beijing, but he has not yet been deigned with a response.

39 bottom right
After the failed
attempt at regaining
independence, the
Tibetan population
underwent various
Chinese attempts
at political
indoctrination
to convince them
to accept Socialist
philosophy.

38-39 In March
1959, the forces of
Tibetan resistance
surrendered to the
Chinese troops, which
quickly put down the

insurrection in Lhasa
in just a few days.

39 bottom left In
1904, the troops of the
British

Younghusband
expedition entered
Lhasa to convince the
Tibetans to negotiate
a commercial treaty
with Britain.

39

PLATEAUS, PEAKS, AND HIGH ALTITUDE DESERT

Traditional Tibet, i.e. the region that lay within the recognized borders until 1959, covered an area of almost one million square miles, equal in size to all of western Europe. It lay almost entirely on a high plateau bordered by China to the north and east, by India to the west, and by India, Nepal, Bhutan, and Burma to the south. The Tibetan plateau lies at an average altitude of a little over 13,000 feet (the reason why it is nicknamed the Roof of the World) which, over the millennia, has discouraged human settlement; indeed, the population of Tibet has never exceeded ten millions.

This endless high altitude expanse is formed by an alternation of empty plains and massive mountain chains whose peaks in various cases exceed 26,000 feet.

The latest research into the geography of the mountains in the region – which are inevitably of major importance in the physical description of the country – have confirmed that the most important ranges (the Himalayas that form the southern border, the Kunlun to the north-west, and the Karakorum to the west) were created following an immense collision some 100 to 50 million years ago between the mass of land that today constitutes India, which had separated from the supercontinent Gondwana, and another continental landmass named Laurasia.

42 top left The
sturdy, untiring yak
is used as a means of
transport, and
nomads drink its
milk and use its skin
to make tents.

42 bottom left In
some eastern areas
of Tibet the high
altitude desert gives
way to forests and
streams.

42 right The
Yamdrok is one of
Tibet's many lakes
that create a strong
contrast with the bare
and harsh landscapes
of the country.

42-43 As soon as
the land permits it,
Tibetan farmers
grow the barley that
constitutes the basis
of their diet.

43 top left Navigable
for much of its course,
the Yarlung Tsangpo
is also used for
communication
purposes.

The area that has historically experienced the greatest development – and where Tibetan civilization originated – is central and western Tibet, which mostly coincides with the current Autonomous Region created by Beijing in 1965 (it measures 463,000 square miles). The other regions of Tibet, Amdo, and Kham make up more than half of the country and have been incorporated into the Chinese provinces of Qingai, Sichuan, and Yunnan. The

43 top right The
Yarlung Tsangpo
(Brahmaputra) cuts
lengthways across
almost all of central
Tibet.

main Tibetan cities lie in the Autonomous Region: Lhasa (the capital), Shigatse, and Gyantse. Here the climate is cold but tolerable in winter, and mild in spring, summer, and autumn. The land is suitable for agriculture and pastureland, and the terrestrial connections with the south are relatively short (even though it is necessary to go over passes between 16,000 and 20,000 feet high in order to cross the Himalayas).

44 top left Massive
chains of mountains
do not just lie to the
south of the Tibet
on the Nepalese and
Indian borders, but
also to the west where
the Qinghai region
extends.

44 top right At times
the Tibetan plateau
is no more than a
sand desert. The
small population of
some regions is the
direct result of the
inhospitality of the
environment.

The area to the west of central Tibet was home for a thousand years or so to the great civilizations of Guge and Purang. In effect, it is a vast high-altitude desert boasting areas of cultivatable and grassy land made possible by the presence of several important rivers that have their sources in this zone. Around Mount Kailash, the four main waterways of the entire Indo-Tibeto-Himalayan region rise: the Ganges, the Indus, the Brahmaputra, and the Sutlej. The Ganges, Indus, and Sutlej immediately head south to enter the sub-continent whereas the Brahma-

44-45 Although the
Chinese have built a
number of
carriageable roads
over the last decades,
the horse and cart
are still used by
Tibetans as a means
of transport.

putra flows west across all of southern Tibet before turning right and cutting through the Himalayas into India. To the north of central Tibet lies the immense Chang Tang plateau. This endless grassland contains no fixed human settlements and is only visited by man during the seasonal migrations of nomadic Tibetans taking their herds to pasture.

45 When the sand
dunes of the high-
altitude deserts ride
up against a sheet
of lake water, the
surreal sight seems
like a mirage.

The substantial differences in altitude and climate in Tibet have created a diversified environment. The Chang Tang plateau is an enormous expanse of grassland without any other type of vegetation, whereas the river areas of central Tibet have many trees (mostly willows and junipers) and different varieties of flowers.

In the zones that border Nepal, the land is rich with pine and fir, and the eastern districts with oak, elm, and birch.

The Tibetan fauna is equally rich and varied even though, because of uncontrolled hunting mainly by Chinese colonists, many species are in danger of extinction. The most characteristic animal of Tibet is the yak, a large and extremely resistant ruminant able to exist at heights of over 19,000 feet. Today it is almost extinct in the wild but the domestic species is very common and used widely in Tibet and the Himalayan region as a beast of burden.

The milk and strongly flavored yogurt that the yak produces are very much appreciated. In addition, Tibetan nomads use the skin of the animal to produce rudimentary but warm coats and the hide for the black tents they live in during their migrations.

Another symbol of Tibet is the snow leopard but today it is very rare. A small and highly skilled feline predator, it lives at an altitude of between 9,500 and 20,000 feet but, when prompted by hunger, will descend to lower levels in search of food.

The few bamboo forests that still exist in eastern Tibet are home to giant pandas, while herds of *chiru* (antelope) and *kyang* (wild donkeys) live in the valleys of central and western Tibet. At higher levels there are groups of *shou* (wild Tibetan deer) but these are now in serious danger of extinction.

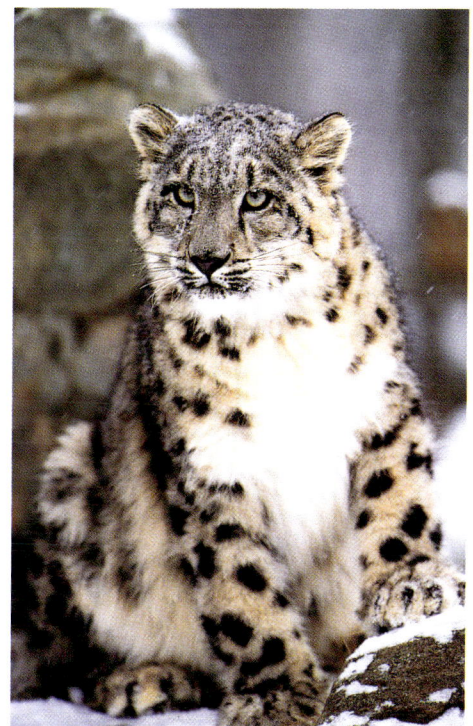

48 top Tibet is famous for the mani, *piles of stones carved with prayers and mantras, that pilgrims build along the roadside and at mountain passes.*

48 center In the areas that receive the most rain, in summer the high-altitude desert is transformed into a green ocean.

48 bottom In Tingri in south Tibet close to the Nepalese border, the grasslands extend way beyond the horizon.

48-49 In the southern areas of the country in particular, the houses and villages have maintained their traditional Tibetan architecture.

49 top left In summer most of the monsoon clouds are halted by the Himalayan chain, but some manage to get through and bring rain to central Tibet.

49 top right Despite the mountain's enormous height, the traveler does not always realize he is passing Everest as it is often hidden by an impenetrable blanket of cloud.

Tibet and Nepal share the world's highest mountains, a ring of peaks of unrivaled beauty that stand over 26,000 feet high. Chomolungma is the Mother Goddess of the Universe that reaches a height of 29,004 feet, but is better known as Mount Everest (named after Sir George Everest, the Englishman who made the first trigonometric survey of it). The mountain was first climbed in 1953 by New Zealander George Hillary and a Nepalese sherpa, Tenzing Norgay. However, despite being the tallest mountain in Tibet, Chomolungma is not the most sacred: this honor goes to Mount Kailash, at only 22,022 feet, that all the peoples of the Tibeto-Himalayan area venerate as the abode of the gods and center of the universe. To Jains, Kailash is the place that the great holy man Rishabha, the first of the 24 Tirthankara, achieved liberation. Hindus believe it to be the mystical paradise where Shiva sits in perennial meditation with his consort Parvati, the daughter of the Himalayas. To followers of the Bon faith, Kailash was the "crystal giant" on which Thonpa Shenrab (the founder of Bon) descended to earth from heaven.

For Tibetan Buddhists, however, Kang Rinpoche (their name for Kailash) is the abode of the Tantric divinity Chakrasamvara and his consort Vajravarahi. It is also associated with the Buddha Sakyamuni, Padmasambhava, and with the greatest mystic in Tibetan history, Milarepa.

50 top left The best
moment to admire
the Himalayan peaks
(this is the Kang
Shung glacier on
Everest) is at dawn
when sudden
clearings in the
clouds provide clear
views.

50 top right The
multicolored prayer
flags give their
blessings to the first
Everest base camp.

50-51 Since it was
first climbed in 1953,
Everest has been
a challenge to
innumerable
climbing expeditions,
but their members do
not always respect the
delicate ecosystem of
the Himalayas.

51 top Everest has
been conquered by
many expeditions
which leave from
both the Nepalese
and Tibetan sides.
Summer and spring
offer the best
climbing weather.

51 bottom Herds of
yak graze at the feet
of the Kang Shung
glacier on the east
face of Everest, as they
have always done.
They are the only
animals able to
tolerate this altitude.

52-53 Small lakes,
iced over almost all
year round, lie at
very high altitudes
in the Himalayas,
like this one at
19,250 feet that
reflects the peaks
of Everest.

The sources of the four great rivers of Asia are all located within 60 miles of this mountain: the Indus to the north, the Brahmaputra to the east, the Karnali (one of the main tributaries of the Ganges) to the south, and the Sutlej to the west. Pilgrims travel to Kailash from India, Tibet, and the whole Himalayan region. Most of them arrive on foot exhausted after arduous journeys lasting weeks or months, but they are happy. They bathe in the crystalline and freezing waters of lakes Manasarovar and Raksas Tal that ring the mountains, they prostrate themselves in homage to the triangular profile of the mountain, and, in three or four days, complete the ritual circle around the base of the mountain on foot (32 miles).

The shores of Marasarovar and Raksas Tal are a crossroads of Asia where Tibetan nomads, families of Jain merchants, Hindu *sadhus,* hermits, high-ranking Buddhist lamas, simple monks from monasteries across Tibet, middle-class families from Delhi, Mumbai, and Kolkota, and farmers from all parts of Tibet converge on this spiritual crucible. They are of different faiths, speak different languages and belong to social and cultural worlds that often have nothing in common, but they are a mosaic of individuals and groups who, in the shadow of the "Venerable Jewel," find a point of contact in the unfathomable mystery of faith.

54 top Seen from the Tibetan valleys in the clear air, the Himalayas can be observed in all their grandeur.

54 bottom On winter days, the white Himalayan peaks stand out above the bare expanse of the Tibetan plateau and against the cobalt blue sky.

54-55 Dawn colors the peaks of Lhotse and Everest.

55 top left At an average altitude of 16,000 feet, yak are the only animals able to cross the snowy expanses of Tibet in winter.

55 top right As soon as spring arrives, the ice of the mountain streams melts and yak can once more drink their water.

56 top left Some Tibetan Buddhists make their pilgrimage to Mount Kailash while performing a ceaseless series of prostrations that makes their journey last years.

56 top right Of all the sacred mountains in the Himalayas, Kailash is the most venerated. It is an object of devotion for the Buddhist, Hindu, and Bon religions.

56-57 Mount Kailash, known as Gang Rinpoche (Jewel of the Snows) to Tibetans, is the most sacred mountain in the Himalayas. Though it is "only" 22,022 feet high, it is known as the "House of the Gods."

57 top Many Buddhist and Hindu monasteries lie in the area around Kailash. They are inhabited by few monks and provide pilgrims with refreshment and sustenance.

57 bottom Not even the intense cold and snow dissuade the faithful from performing their exhausting pilgrimage to Mount Kailash.

58 top During
summer when the
monsoon winds
manage to pass over
the Himalayan
chain, the mountains
along the Yarlung
river are almost
always shrouded
in cloud.

58 bottom The boats
that navigate the
Yarlung are still one
of the pilgrims' main
means of transport.

58-59 The
abundant summer
rains swell the river
Yarlung and often
turn its banks into
high-altitude
marshes.

59 top left Small
isolated hermitages
on the peak of a
mountain are made
visible by streams of
colored flags and
offer an unspoiled
sanctuary for prayer.

59 top right In July and August, if the monsoons from the south are particularly strong, rain around the Yarlung forms streams of water that make travel difficult.

60 top left The heavy
rain clouds that
darken the sky in
summer create
marvelous effects
of the light.

60 top right and 60-
61 When the rains
are insistent, the
Tibetan landscape
is transformed,
sometimes resembling
the countryside of
Southeast Asia.

61 top There are
no bridges over the
Yarlung and boats
are the only way to
ford it. Crossing is
unpleasant when the
river is swollen by the
summer rains.

61 center To the south
of Mount Kailash
lies the large lake,
Manasarovar, which,
at 14,954 feet, is one
of the highest in the
world and held sacred
by Hindus and
Buddhists.

61 bottom Gray
clouds and the
immensity of the
Himalayan range
are characteristic
of summer in Tibet.

62 top left The Chinese influence is dramatically evident in the modern buildings constructed in Lhasa, which often dwarf masterpieces of Tibetan architecture.

62 top right Even in modern city development, some link with Tibetan tradition is attempted, such as in these two enormous gilded yaks.

62-63 Although modern constructions represent 60 percent of the buildings in Lhasa today, the Potala remains the symbol of the city.

63 left The development of modern Lhasa is very recent, dating from the late twentieth century, and was designed to provide accommodation for the increasing number of Chinese inhabitants.

63 top right and bottom Chinese women in the streets of Lhasa prefer to dress in Western style, whereas Tibetan women opt for their traditional costume.

L hasa – the abode of the gods and capital of the Land of the Snows – is the heart and soul of Tibet. As recently as the early 1950's it was still a small, medieval city of barely 21,000 inhabitants, near which stood the three largest Tibetan monasteries. It was the center of an archaic society that had deliberately chosen to turn its back on material progress and concentrate its energies on inner knowledge and spiritual development.

Lhasa was once thought a small jewel of Tibetan architecture and art. Tens of thousands of men and women arrived each year from all over Tibet to prostrate themselves and pray before its gods, altars, and temples.

At that time, Lhasa was for the most part made up of two districts: a small village named Shol that lay right below the Potala, and a series of old buildings and narrow alleys around the Jokhang and Ramoché temples.

top The Barkor
is a four-sided
devotional path
around the Jokhang
and still the heart
of Tibetan Lhasa.
Countless Tibetans
follow its path
each day.

64-65 In spite of the
changes of recent
years, the gilded roofs
of the Jokhang and
the pulsing life of the
market still represent
the spirit of Lhasa.

To pass from one side of the city to the other it was necessary to cross a small stone and wood bridge called Yutok Sampa (the Bridge of the Turquoise Roof).

Since 1985, the Chinese have made many architectural alterations and constructed modern buildings that have notably changed the face of Lhasa.

Today, to get an idea of the atmosphere of the old city, almost the only place to visit is the old, Tibetan district, especially the quarter of the Barkhor around the Jokhang. Here the tangled streets are lined with traditional, two-story masonry houses, lined on the outside with lime, with rectangular windows outlined in black, wide yards, porches, and sturdy doors framed by multicolored baroque patterns.

Barkhor was once a colorful bazaar filled with people and noise that wound through the narrow, crowded streets (perhaps the only place in traditional Tibet that had ever been congested). It was a market, a permanent fair, and place to meet and chat.

In 641, when the Jokhang was constructed, a small street called the Barkhor was also built for the ritual circumambulation and, over the centuries, a small district grew up around it. Today the modern Chinese buildings, often brutally ugly, have destroyed many of their

65 top The typical multicolored Chinese umbrellas stand on the sides of the Tibetan pilgrims who circumambulate the Jokhang.

65 top center The smoke of the juniper branches burned in tribute to the gods is a constant in Tibetan religious life.

65 bottom center You can find almost anything in the sea of stalls in the Barkhor, but rarely anything of real value.

65 bottom This Tibetan man is purifying his karma by turning his mani khorlo (the long staff topped by a brass wheel which contains prayer sheets).

traditional counterparts, the stark-
est example being the dozens de-
molished in front of the Jokhang to
make way for a dull, graceless
square.

Nonetheless, the Barkhor still
retains some of its traditional atmosphere and wandering among its
small shops and busy stalls remains
a pleasurable experience.

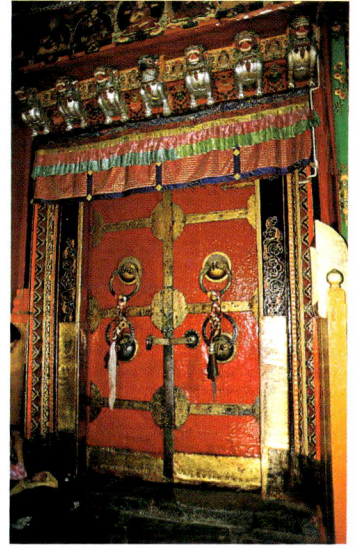

Buddha (the one of the Jowo Sakyamuni that was brought from China by Princess Wen Cheng, one of Songtsen Gampo's wives, is particularly important), of Tzonghkapa, Padmasambhava, Avalokitesvara, the Buddha of Medicine, and many other gods and Buddhist saints. They stop for a moment, their hands joined and eyes closed, and place their offerings on the altar (almost always lamps filled with melted butter and a burning wick) before passing on to the next altar and next offering.

The air is filled with a mixture of the bitter smell of the butter and the sweet perfume of incense. Prayers and mantras are chanted in all the dialects of Tibet and the deep beat of ritual drums played by monks in the little chapels at the sides of the main room merge with the footsteps of the crowd and the pilgrims' exclamations of amazement at the abundance of sacred images.

The unique brand of religious feeling in the Tibetan world is expressed in the Jokhang in all its many-sided contradictoriness.

The supernatural is characteristic of this part of the world, and here it mixes with the sophisticated elegance of Buddhist philosophy. Simple, everyday faith, yearning after a spiritual dimension encounters and merges with rituals filled with psychological significance.

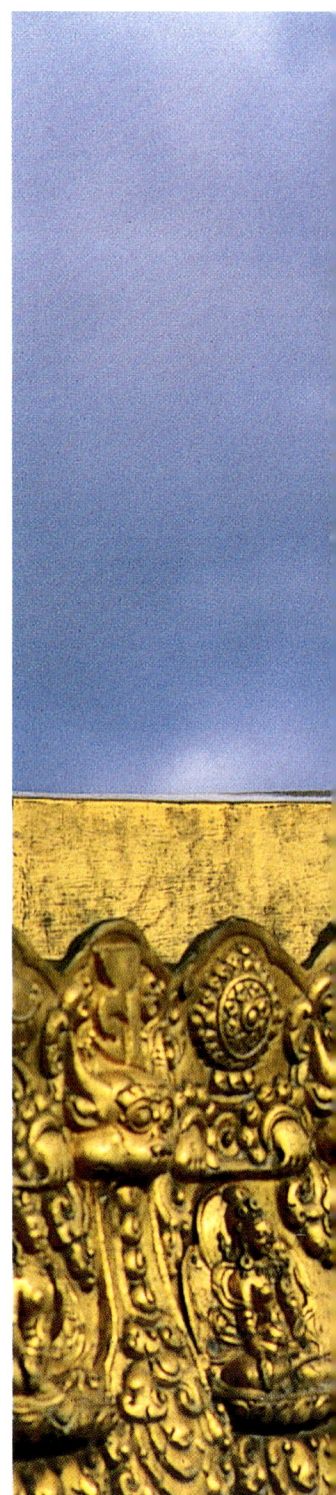

Hundreds of small votive lights illuminate the gloom of the temples to let the worshiper find his way in the Jokhang. The temple was built by Songtsen Gampo in the seventh century and remains the most important in Lhasa and the spiritual heart of Tibet.

This superb religious complex contains splendid, elegant, and opulent examples of Tibetan art. Lines of pilgrims pass before statues of the

70 left The altars in Jokhang Temple are literally covered with ancient statues of the most important Buddhist masters.

70 right The large statue of Padmasambhava – the great Tantric yogi who introduced Buddhism to Tibet in the eight century – is one of the Jokhang's most important works of art.

71 top Pilgrims to monasteries often place their offerings of money in the hands of the statues on the altars.

71 center left Ceremonial hats are distinctive signs of the various Buddhist schools in Tibet. The hat on this statue belongs to the Sakya school.

71 center right
Multicolored fabrics
and brocades are
another characteristic
of Tibetan art and
are seen throughout
the monasteries.

71 bottom In the
Jokhang's main
temple, the monks sit
in rows on either side
of the high altar
during religious
ceremonies.

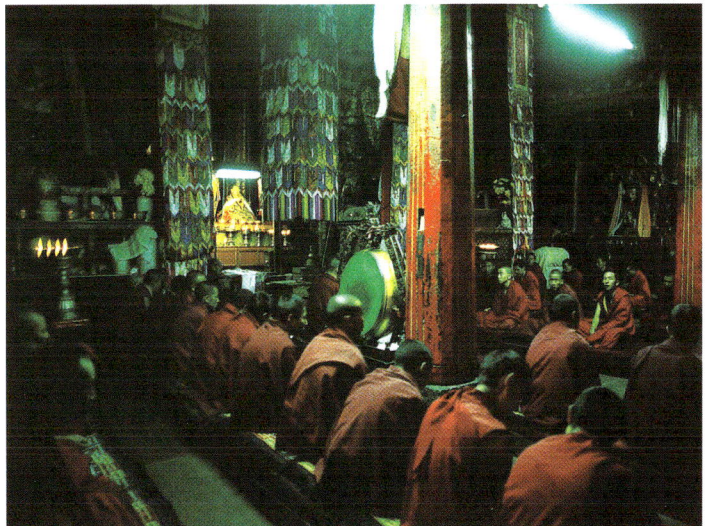

72 top The dozens, sometimes hundreds, of votive lamps that are lit in Jokhang Temple render the atmosphere more evocative.

72 bottom The columns in the monasteries, like these in the Jokhang, whether made of wood or stone, are always inlaid and painted in bright colors.

72-73 This elderly monk is reading religious texts that have been hand-printed on rectangular sheets of paper.

73 top left Offerings of light to the gods are sometimes made with the use of enormous lamps filled with melted yak butter.

73 top right The richness and abundance of ornamentation in Tibet have led to its sacred art being termed "Asiatic Baroque."

POTALA:
THE HEART OF TIBET

The 13 floors of the imposing building of the Potala dominate the valley and city of Lhasa at 380 feet high, and can be seen from tens of miles away. Indeed, if one arrives in Lhasa by land, it is the only means of knowing how close to the Tibetan capital you are. The Potala was and still is the symbol of Tibet. The name of the palace is derived from the name of a mountain in southern India that Buddhists consider sacred to the *bodhisattva* Chenrezig, and the palace itself is rightly considered one of the greatest architectural treasures in Asia. It is so large that no one knows for sure how many rooms it has. Until 1959, it contained the residence of the Dalai Lama, a monastery, dozens of chapels (each dedicated to a particular god of Tantric Buddhism), government offices, and other components. It was the heart of Tibet and the religious, social, and cultural point of reference for the entire country. Each morning and evening, the inhabitants of Lhasa along with the many pilgrims (who arrived in great numbers, especially for New Year celebrations) would perform the ritual walk around the palace, their hands joined in prayer and eyes turned towards the rooms where the Dalai Lama lived. The most devout would circle the palace performing the ritual prostration until they completed the circumference (nearly a mile). It was an act of homage, devotion, and inner purifica-tion that received the full respect of the Tibetan people.

In the changed political situation today, everything is different. Although it was prohibited outright at the start of the 1980's, the circum-ambulation of the Potala is once again permitted and Tibetans, at sunrise and sunset, continue to perform the ritual even if the Dalai Lama no longer resides behind the high walls. To all effects, the Potala is now a museum that anyone can visit, whether Tibetan or tourist, and, to the foreigner, the families of local pilgrims

become even more appealing as they wander a little lost around the sacred palace of the "Precious Protector."

After climbing the flight of stone steps, visitors begin to wander the many rooms and chapels with a certain weariness. Those worthy of mention are the Chapel of Maitreya, the Chapel of the three-dimensional Mandala, the tomb of the thirteenth Dalai Lama, the Chapel of Kalachakra, and the Chapel of the tombs of the Dalai Lamas. Men and women of all ages and background tiptoe through these rooms that were once prohibited to common folk. They now come from every corner of Tibet, light lamps in the chapels open to the public, prostrate themselves in front of the altars, the statues of the gods, and the *chorten* that contain the remains of earlier Dalai Lamas, and they pray. They pray everywhere, fingering their rosaries and turning the prayer wheels. They pray as they walk, while they wait in line to enter a room, and while they wait for their friends. They pray to their gods, their masters, their Buddhas. Above all, they pray that one day the "Presence" can return to reside in the place that, to their eyes, is the heart of the Roof of the World.

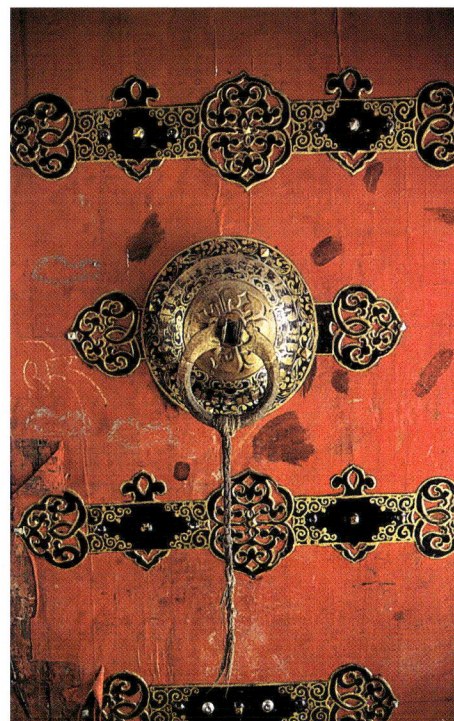

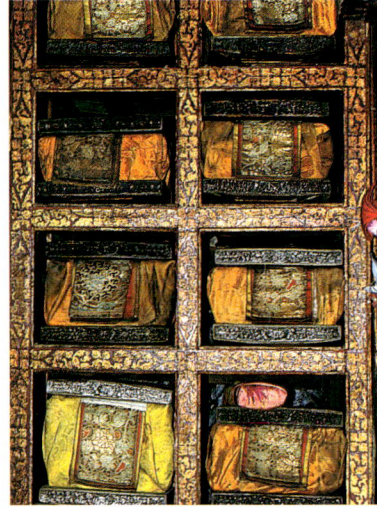

78 top left The walls
of the Potala, like
those in most Tibetan
monasteries, are
painted with religious
subjects to emphasize
the profound
spirituality of
the place.

78 top right The
rectangular sheets
of religious books are
squeezed between
planks, then bound
with colored cotton
or brocade strips,
and finally placed
in these libraries.

78-79 and 79 bottom
Wandering through
the rooms of the
Potala is a fantastic
experience. The visitor
is literally stunned
by the richness and
colorfulness of the
decorations.

79 top Besides being
objects of worship,
the many altars in
the Potala are also
the artistic expressions
of a culture that is
highly religious.

Two miles from the center of Lhasa lies the Norbu Linka. This set of palaces and chapels was built as a summer residence by Jampel Gyatso, the eighth Dalai Lama, where a small wood stood in the eighteenth century. In spring, the spiritual and temporal rulers of Tibet would leave the Potala and transfer to Norbu Linka followed by a long procession. All Lhasa turned out into the streets to watch the sacred parade, as well as pilgrims who used to travel from the remotest regions of Tibet and suffer inconveniences of all sorts just to be present at this wonderful event at least once in their lives.

The main palaces in Norbu Linka were built by the eighth, thirteenth, and fourteenth Dalai Lamas. The residence of Tagtu Migyur Podrang (the fourteenth) has since been turned into a museum and is now an obligatory stop on the itineraries of every self-respecting travel agency.

80 top left The Norbulingka stands a few miles from the Potala; it was the Dalai Lama's summer palace when he governed Tibet.

80 top right The Norbulingka was originally built as a summer palace but was soon enlarged to accommodate the entire governmental apparatus.

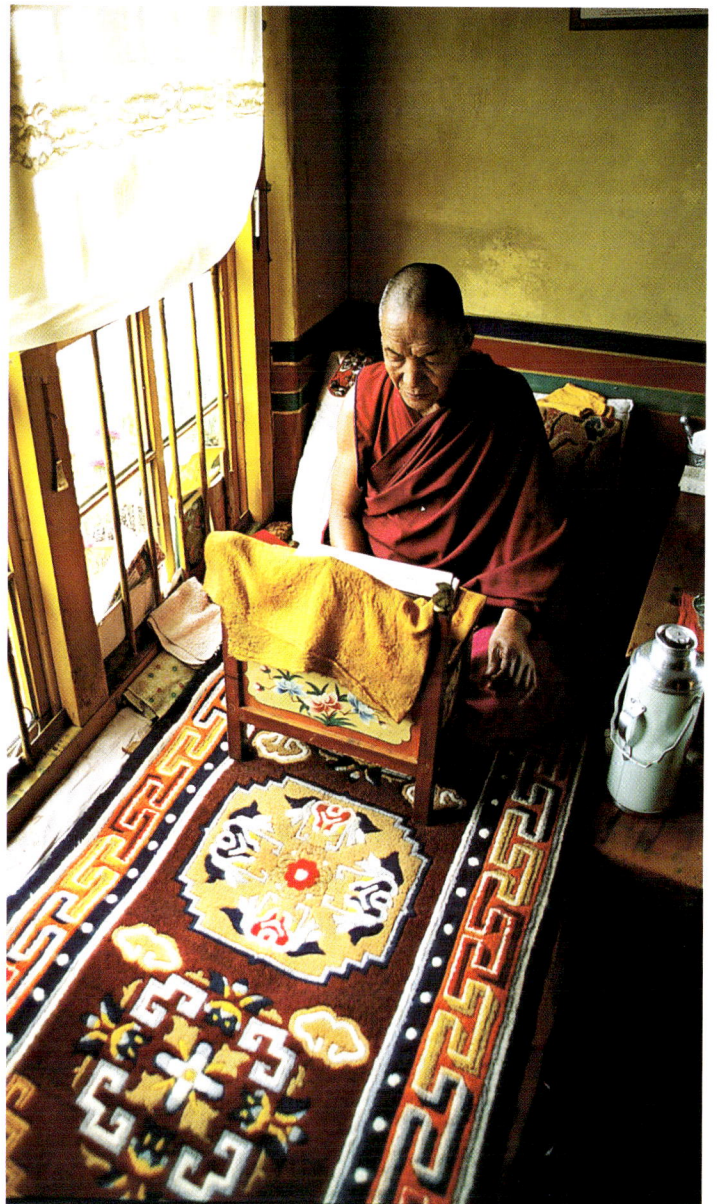

80-81 Much smaller and less imposing than the Potala, the Norbulingka (this is the entrance) is more intimate and modest.

81 top It was from the Norbulingka that the Dalai Lama fled to India. Since his departure, his rooms have not been touched.

81 bottom Some monks have remained in the Norbulingka, though today the complex is a public museum.

82 top left Sera Monastery, near Lhasa, is one of the most important study centers in Tibet.

82 center left Music plays a fundamental role in ritual ceremonies.

82 bottom left The numerous statues of spiritual masters on Tibetan altars are not indicative of idolatry but a symbol that reminds the devotee of the principle of Enlightenment that is present in every human being.

82 bottom right Bronze and gold are the materials used to make images of the Buddhist gods more dramatic.

82-83 Like the walls of the most important monasteries and palaces in Tibet, those in one of the monastic colleges at Sera are slightly inclined and have black-framed windows.

Built at the foot of a tall hill, Sera monastery stands only three miles from the center of Lhasa and can be seen from the terraces of the Potala and other points in the city. Founded in 1419 by Shakya Yeshe– one of the most important disciples of Lama Tzong Khapa–, the monastery accommodated up to 6,000 monks until the 1950's; today there are only a few more than 300. The most interesting of the buildings in the complex is the Sera-Me College in whose numerous chapels there are important works of art, such as the statue of the Buddha Sakyamuni. This is known as the "Miwang Jowo" because it was commissioned in the fifteenth century by the Miwang family. Other important statues are those of the first, second, third, and fifth Dalai Lamas. The oldest building, the Tantric College, is also very attractive, and the capitals on the columns in the Entrance Room are among the most elegant in Tibet. Slightly more recent is the Sera-Je College where chapels hold a large number of altars and the statues of Tzong Khapa, Buddha Sakyamuni, Manjusri, and Jamchen Chöje, the founder of Sera.

About five miles from the center of Lhasa, the monastery of Drepung was built in 1416 by another of Lama Tzong Khapa's important disciples, Jamyang Tashi Pelden. It is said that before the arrival of the Chinese, Drepung was the largest monastery in the world with its 8,000 resident monks. One of its loveliest buildings, Ganden Palace, was the residence of the second, third, fourth, and fifth Dalai Lamas before the central body of the Potala was completed.

84 top right In Buddhist symbolism, the wheel represents the Buddha's preachings.

84-85 Before the Chinese occupation of Tibet, Drepung was the largest monastery in the world. Some of it has been restored and monastic life continues today, though to a much more limited extent.

85 top Over the centuries, Drepung suffered onslaughts from the Tsang monarchs and the Mongols.

85 bottom In traditional Tibet, Drepung was renowned for the splendor of its paintings and frescoes.

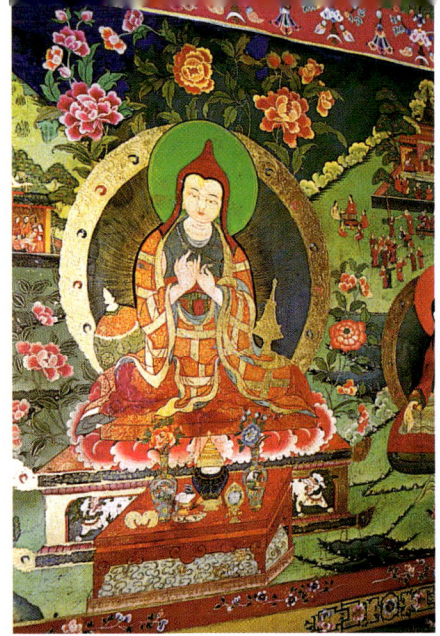

86 bottom left A thousand-armed statue of Avalokitesvara, who symbolizes the principle of compassion, protects the statue of the founder of the Gelug school, Lama Tzong Khapa.

86 top left The light offered by worshipers still brightens the altars of Drepung and the statues of the Buddha.

Today Drepung hosts only 200 monks. In the Main Assembly Room there is a chapel dedicated to the Buddha Sakyamuni with statues of the Buddha himself, Maitreya, Kasyapa, and the Buddha's two principal disciples, Shariputra and Maudgalyayana. There are also nine *stupa* of Kalachakra and images of the Eight Great Bodhisattvas and the irate divinities Vajrapani and Hayagriva. The chapel built by Tzong Khapa in the Tantric College is of special interest. Tzong Khapa also promoted the carving of the statue of Yamantaka, which is still present on the high altar. Statues of Tzong Khapa and several Dalai Lamas are also to be seen in the large Assembly Room in the Tantric College.

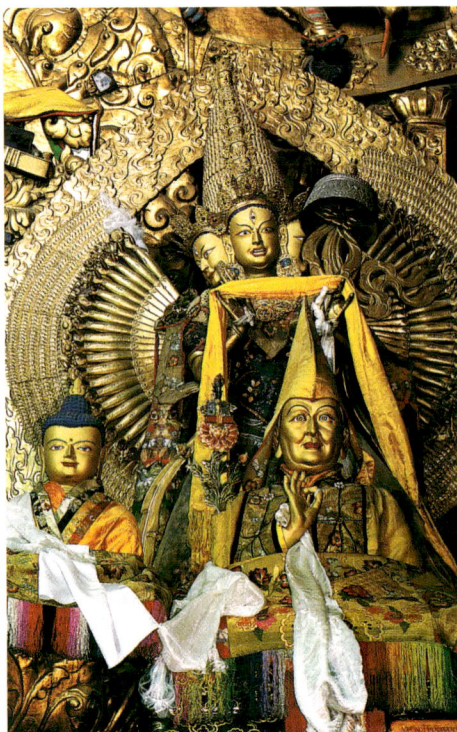

86 top right
Buddhist teachings
are not always
written or spoken
but are also
communicated
through gestures of
the hands, as seen
in this fresco in
Drepung.

86-87 These colored
silk and brocade
ornaments hang
from the ceiling of
the Assembly Room
in Drepung
Monastery.

87 top In the
darkness of Drepung's
temples, the light of
the votive candles is
often the only means
of seeing the statues
on the altars.

87 bottom The large
prayer-wheels in
Drepung, as in the
other monasteries,
require cumbersome
maintenance
operations.

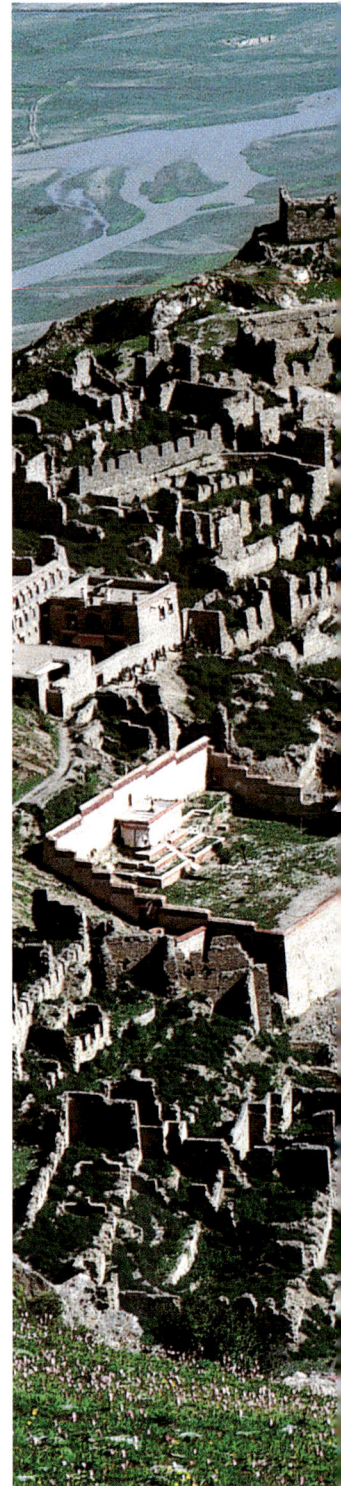

Built like an amphitheater on the peak of a mountain roughly 25 miles from Lhasa, Ganden monastery may have been the most beautiful in all Tibet. Also founded by Lama Tzong Khapa in 1417, Ganden (the name means "Pure Land") is one of the most sacred places in the Gelug school of Buddhism as it is the burial place of Tzong Khapa.

Unfortunately, Ganden was razed to the ground during the Cultural Revolution, and today the Tibetans have managed to rebuild only a few buildings and meditation rooms of the original complex that housed 6,000 monks.

Those places that retain a certain artistic value are the Gold Tomb of Lama Tzong Khapa (once one of the masterpieces of Tibet), the chapel dedicated to Dharmaraja, and what remains of the *chorten* that contains the remains of Lama Tzong Khapa.

MONASTERIES: THE FORTRESSES OF THE MAHAYANA

90-91 Mandalas made from colored sand are complex meditative patterns made by monks for particular ceremonies. At the end of the ceremony, the mandala is destroyed.

91 top left Aspiring monks are entered into monasteries very young (at about six years of age) as trapa (novices) by their families.

91 top right It is only possible to become a gelong (monk) after reaching legal age and after demonstrating deep personal conviction.

90 bottom Some Tibetan monasteries are famous for the excellent quality of the sacred books that they print. They use wooden blocks inlaid by hand over which they pass cloths soaked in ink. The block is then pressed onto sheets of rice paper.

Although there have been numerous examples of spiritual teachings being passed on by lay masters outside monastic centers, it was in the monasteries themselves that Tibetan Buddhism found the most suitable means of preserving itself and evolving. From small centers to the large monastic cities where thousands of monks lived, *gompa* (monasteries) represented the heart of Tibeto-Himalayan civilization. The *gompa* has always been and will continue to be, where political conditions permit, the "highest" point of reference for Buddhist peoples. In a world where the sacred was so universally present, the monastery was the pre-eminent center of religious function. Internally, the monks celebrated, on behalf of the entire community, the rituals and liturgies performed to benefit not only the officiators but the whole of society. Architecturally, the Buddhist monastic complexes of Tibet and the entire Himalayan region blend perfectly into the landscape and are harmoniously joined to the natural environment through colors and materials. The most remarkable aesthetic features are the white walls with the black-framed rectangular windows, the wooden balconies on the upper floors, and the roofs, generally terraced and adorned with decorations or ornamental motifs. The spiritual center of the monastery often lay at the physical center of the complex: the *sancta sanctorum* of the entire complex, the central temple, a three-story building, was known as the *lha-khang* (house of the gods). It con-

tained altars, sculptures and paintings of the gods, offerings, and ritual objects. The *lha-khang* can vary a great deal in size but must be either square or rectangular in shape; in this case the altar stands in the center of the shortest wall opposite the entrance gate.

The *du-khang* (meeting house) is a large room where liturgical ceremonies and monks' assemblies are held. It contains an altar on one wall in front of which are laid out the long lines of cushions on which the monks sit. The seats of the *tulku* (reincarnated lamas such as the abbot, the "Masters of Ceremony," and others) stand in front of the cushions in order of significance. Another important place is the *gon-khang*, which is the small chapel that contains the statues of the guardian deities of the monastery, portrayed in their terrifying aspect. The *gon-khang* can be situated in its own building or on the upper floors of the *lha-khang*.

The *zimchung* is the room where the highest-ranking lama, generally a *tulku*, resides. The *zimchung* is usually located inside the main temple building with its window overlooking the courtyard. The monks live in cells, the size of which de-

pends on the wealth of the monastery. They are usually small rooms with a bed, an altar for private devotions, and a corner for cooking. As the ritual circumambulation of sacred places is an important aspect of Buddhist worship, monasteries often have a sort of internal corridor built for this very purpose, which may be just a dark and comfortless passageway in which the air hardly moves. On occasions, however, the route is outdoors, often a roofed path that winds around the main building with a row of prayer-wheels on the right that the worshiper spins as he circles the temple. The

courtyard has an important function in the life of the monastery. It is where the monks study religious texts and hold philosophical debates, and where the lamas confer their teachings when the crowds cannot be accomodated in the *du-khang*. The courtyard is also used for the *cham*, the important ritual Tantric dances that are one of the most important expressions of the religion and culture of Tibetan Buddhism. Spirituality invests every aspect of life in Tibetan society. The importance of the monk has no equal. The prestige that surrounds his figure is remarkable; before the Chi-

nese invasion, parents usually attempted to steer at least one of their male children towards a religious career. In the 1940's there were more than 750,000 monks out of a population of roughly six million. Only a few were capable of reaching the highest ranks of the monastic hierarchy, but every monk would benefit from the dignity that flowed from belonging to such an important institution. Before the occupation, there were thousands of monasteries in Tibet, but in the period following 1959, and particularly during the Cultural Revolution (1966-1976), most of them were either shut or destroyed. However, in the changed political situation in China today, hundreds of *gompa* are once again active in Tibet. Tibetan monasteries are similar in structure. The head of the community is the *trindzin* (head abbot), who has reached this position as a result of his spiritual achievements or because he is considered the reincarnation of the previous abbot. The *trindzin* is helped by the *gyaltsap* (ruling abbot), who is the monastery's second highest authority. The *kempo* (master of studies) is a figure of great erudition whose task it is to teach the most important religious subjects. Other positions include the *dorje lopon*, the lama in charge of celebrating the Tantric rites, the *drupon*, the master of meditation, the *umdze*, who directs the chanting and musical performances of the monastery's band, and the *chopon*, who is responsible for the maintenance of the altars and votive offerings.

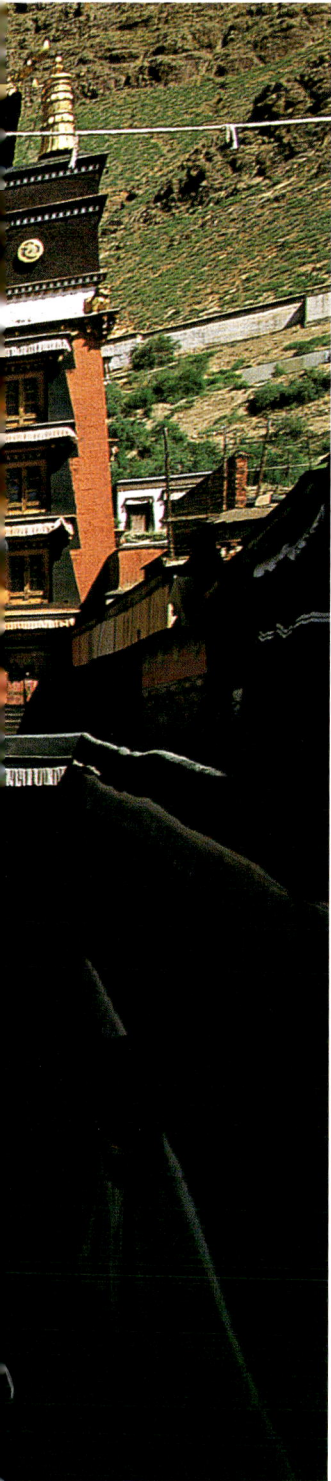

One of the most interesting and typical aspects of Tibetan monasticism is the education and training of the monks. When a child enters the monastery he is a *trapa* (novice), a status he retains until he reaches the age of maturity, about 18, when he is able to decide whether to take vows and become a *gelong* (full monk). In other words, the decision to become a *gelong* is taken by the *trapa* alone and is not affected by the wishes of his family.

Generally, novices enter the monastery between the ages of six and ten. Once he is there, he finds he is confronted by a contradictory situation. On the one hand, there is the encounter with a prestigious institution, its rituals and communal moments, and authoritative (rarely authoritarian) masters whose preferred facial expression is a smile. On the other hand, there is the trauma of the boy's separation from his known world, his family, and, in particular, from his mother who in any case attempts to keep the boy in the monastery though remaining close to him until he has become accustomed to his new situation.

The boys begin their educational program immediately upon arrival, starting with writing and grammar, and including the study of complex Buddhist texts that would not usually be present in Western curriculums until late high school or university. The monastery is also the residence of most of the *rinpoche* (precious masters), men who have succeeded in achieving total

spiritual liberation but who have renounced *nirvana* in order to return to Earth in a sequence of reincarnations to aid others with the power of their wisdom. Tibetans venerate these masters so greatly that words are difficult to find to describe their respect. Recognized when they are children as reincarnations of earlier *rinpoche*, the boys are brought up (usually as monks) with great care by highly qualified tutors and teachers. Once their studies end and they reach adulthood, they once more perform the tasks of spiritual guidance that is their real reason for existence in the

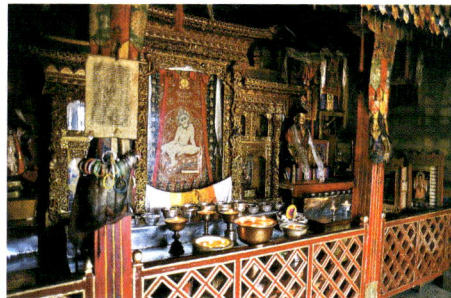

material world. There are thousands of "precious masters" in Tibetan tradition. The most important is unquestionably the Dalai Lama, the living symbol of the Land of the Snows, followed by the Panchen Lama and the Karmapa. Whereas some of the other *rinpoche* are also famous and are venerated across Tibet, some are only known in the areas where they live. Nevertheless, Tibetans consider all of them to be manifestations of the highest levels of spirituality and religiousness.

97 top left The layout of Samye Monastery symbolizes the universe with a temple at its center around which the other buildings are arranged to form two concentric circles.

97 top right Samye is the location of the eighth-century stela on which Trisong Deutsen had the edict carved that proclaimed Buddhism to be Tibet's state religion.

96 top After the restorations of the past few years, Samye has once again become one of the holiest places in Tibet.

96 bottom As the first Buddhist monastery to have been built in Tibet, Samye belongs without distinction to all the schools of Tibetan Buddhism.

96-97 Prayer flags disperse into the air the beneficial power of sacred formulas but also soften the massive face of Samye Monastery with their colors.

The monastery of Samye stands on the bank of the river Tsang-Po (Brahmaputra to the Indians) about 25 miles from the town of Tsetang. It was founded in 763 by King Trison Deutsen and Padmasambhava and was the first Buddhist monastery to be built in Tibet. Samye is still considered one of the most important places of pilgrimage in all of Tibet and it is visited by large numbers of people from all over the country. They arrive alone or in groups, both laymen and monks, to meditate, pray, and prostrate themselves on the soil that was once blessed by the presence of this "precious master" and his most important disciples. Pilgrims and travelers are impressed on their arrival by a stele inscribed in 799 displaying the edict by which Trison Deutsen proclaimed Buddhism the official state religion and by a large bell suspended from the beams of an entrance arch to the ceremonial room. The layout of the original complex was an expression of the Buddhist cosmology with a central temple representing Mount Sumeru, the mythical mountain at the center of the universe, and four other temples (called *ling*) representing the four continents that lay in the vast ocean to the north, south, east, and west of Mount Sumeru. To the right and left of each temple there were two smaller ones, *ling-tren*, that represented the subcontinents of the Buddhist cosmology, and two small chapels embodied the sun and the moon. The perimeter was surrounded by a long round wall and four large *stupa*, each a different color (white, red, blue, and green) placed at the cardinal points of the compass.

During the Cultural Revolution, Samye suffered greatly and few of the original buildings remained standing at the end of the 1970's. Various buildings have since been repaired and restored (though rather hastily) and now at least the central temple is useable for purposes of worship. There are statues and altars dedicated to the most important schools of Tibetan Buddhism and its principal exponents: Padmasambhava, Atisha, Drom Tönpa, Longchenpa, Sakya Pandita, and Lama Tzong Khapa to mention a few.

The public can be present at the many ritual ceremonies known as *puja* performed by the monks. These ceremonies are mainly carried out in the

shadows touch the crowds. Then, the dancers return to the Tashilunpo's main temple.

About ninety miles from Shigatse heading south-west, there is the monastery of Sakya, the most important center of the Sakya school of Tibetan Buddhism. Founded in 1073 by Konchok Gyalpo, this monastery was a sort of capital for Tibet during the thirteenth and fourteenth centuries when its abbots were conferred with the title of "Governors" of Tibet by the Mongol *khans* and exercised power over all central Tibet.

Unfortunately, many of Sakya's buildings were destroyed during the Cultural Revolution, but the imposing red building of the south monastery remained almost intact. Its enormous prayer hall has large and fine bronze statues of the Buddha Sakyamuni that each contain relics of important Sakya-pa masters. Inside the complex, it is possible to visit the two palaces that at one time were residences of the two main Sakya-pa spiritual lineages. These are the Puntsok Palace, whose main treasures are held in a chapel that contains statues of Tara Bianca, Amitayus, Manjusri, Vijaya, and Lama Sakya Pandita, and the Tara Palace where five superb *stupa* lie in a chapel decorated with excellent frescoes.

Visitors to Sakya can also ob-serve another aspect of Tibetan monastic life closely, that of philosophical debate. During the sessions of this spiritual practice, the normally empty courtyard fills with pairs of monks who challenge one another loudly with religious questions of all types. The monk who asks the question stands and accompanies his query with gestures of his arms and noisy clapping. To press harder on the seated monk whose turn it is to answer, at times the questioner is accompanied by one or two bystanders with the result that the small group will produce almost a chorus of shouts, exclamations, handclaps, and, sometimes, laughter.

The excited gestures and attitudes of the monks give the impression that an altercation, a ballet, or perhaps a demonstration of martial arts is taking place. On the contrary, it is really a sophisticated technique of psychological analysis whose aim is not to defeat one's adversary but to train the mind to operate clearly and, simultaneously, to help one's debating partner to avoid incorrect thinking.

Debating also helps the monks to overcome a limited conception of reality and thus understand the authentic mechanisms that lie at the base of mental dynamics. Therefore, the practice is not a display of academic erudition but an effective method of psychological training.

The small town of Gyantse stands in central Tibet about 160 miles southwest of Lhasa and is perhaps the one that has maintained its tradition of Tibetan civilization most intact. It lies at the foot of a hill where various monasteries used to stand before the Cultural Revolution and is famous for the Kum Bum, or the 100,000 images. It is an imposing construction filled with innumerable altars that contain images of the pantheon of Tantric gods. Built in 1440 by King Rabten Kunsang, the Kum Bum is a five-story building vaguely in the shape of a pagoda with four large pairs of eyes belonging to the Buddha painted on the outside of the upper section. The entire body of the monument is studded with 120 or so large and small chapels.

The Kum Bum is a *chorten,* one of the most characteristic of Tibetan religious buildings. *Chorten* is a Tibetan term that means "receptacle for worship"; it originated in India, where it is called a *stupa,* as a funerary monument built to contain relics of the Buddha Sakyamuni and other great masters. Soon, however, the structure was imbued with other functions: it was sometimes used for complex, esoteric symbolism linked to Buddhist cosmology, or it may have been transformed into a cenotaph built to commemorate a particular event or to increase the spiritual merits of those who built or commissioned it. There are eight types of *chorten* that are differentiated by their architectural form and symbolic

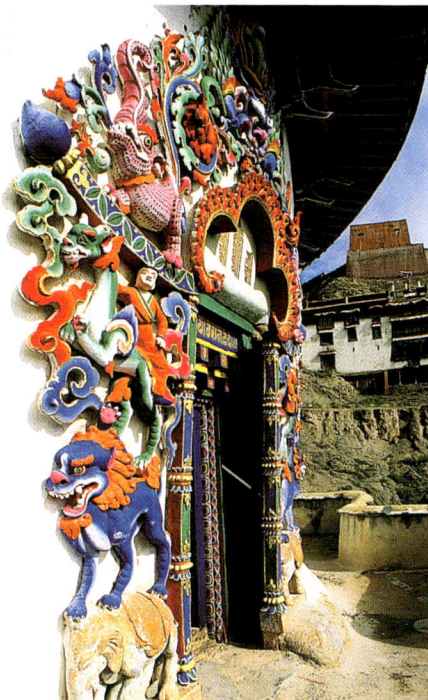

significances. The variations are minimal and often escape the untrained eye as they do not affect the underlying structure, which is the same for all types. Three steps support a square base called the "throne" on which four more steps lead to a dome called the "pot." This forms the base for a reliquary or bushel adorned by thirteen "wheels," and above each wheel is the "triple crown" composed of a crescent moon, a sun, and a disk. The various elements of the *chorten* symbolize their constituent elements: the land, water, fire, air, and ether. *Chorten* are found throughout the Tibeto-Himalayan world, standing either alone or in groups, in cities, on the sides of mountains, in valleys, or at the entrance to towns and villages.

Whatever its function, whether a reliquary, a receptacle for offerings, or a cenotaph, it is certain that the *chorten* is one of the strongest characteristics of Tibetan civilization. It is a symbol of faith, an object of devotion (to be walked around counterclockwise), a motive for introspection, and a subject of religion. The *chorten* exists to remind humanity of the mystery of existence and the uninterrupted cycle of birth-death-rebirth that binds us to a fate marked by ignorance and sorrow.

The Kum Bum is the great *chorten* in Gyantse and another of the most important places of pilgrimage in Tibet. Visiting it brings one into contact with the profound spirituality of the Land of the Snows. Women and men prostrate themselves before its main entrance, walk round it ritually, enter its chapels to pray, light votive lamps, and burn incense. It should be remembered that people do not pay tribute to statues of the lamas and gods for banal reasons of idolatry as is often thought, but rather because they believe the statues are the symbol of the principle of enlightenment present in every human being and that the act of devotion is a bridge built between the devotee and his or her enlightened mind.

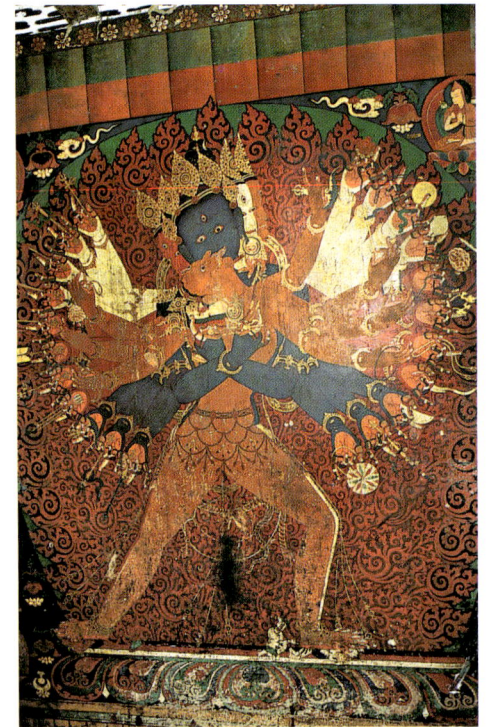

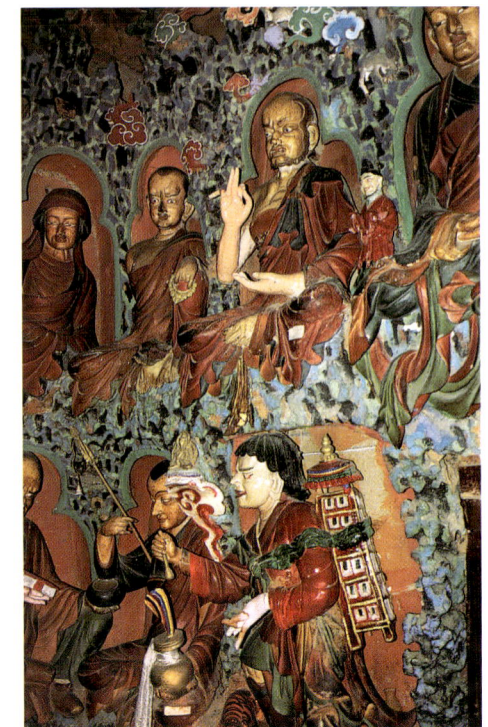

114 top left Losar (the New Year festival) is celebrated in Lhasa with great ostentation and is unquestionably the most important event of the year.

114 top right An enormous tanka is carried by a procession of monks and worshipers before it is displayed.

114-115 The entire monastic community in Nechung Monastery, near Drepung, is involved in the New Year celebrations.

115 top Large religious ceremonies with the participation of monks and laymen are held throughout Tibet during Losar.

115 bottom New Year celebrations include many dance rituals, which are one of the most interesting aspects of Tibetan spirituality.

*U*p until the tragic events of 1959, the traditional Tibetan year was filled with innumerable festivals marking the daily life of the people. Whether religious or secular, large or small, or celebrated in the monasteries or villages, these festivals were a fundamental feature of the culture and civilization of Tibet. In Lhasa, the religious and political capital, the festivals were celebrated most extravagantly, and those wishing to participate in them would travel from the farthest corners of the country on journeys that might take months. With the exception of the third month, the twelve months of the year into which the Tibetan lunar year is divided all included many festivities celebrating the birth, enlightenment, and attainment of nirvana by the Buddha Sakyamani, the payment of homage to the most important gods in the Buddhist pantheon, the commemoration of the kings of Tibet, the veneration of particular astrological conjunctions, and others. The life of the people in the Land of the Snows, however materially deprived it may have been, was at least cheered by dozens of festivals and, as the proverb goes, holy days are holidays. Highly formal ceremonies alternated with relaxed festivities in which large quantities of food and alcoholic drinks (reserved only for members of the lay community) were enjoyed in a joyful atmosphere. Both solemn prayer ceremonies and light-hearted picnics in the parks resulted in the involvement of the entire population, both high and low-

born, laymen and monks, men and women, elderly and children alike. The Chinese occupation of the country and, in particular, the dreadful decade of the Cultural Revolution (1966-1976) led to the ban of every sort of celebration, and it was only in 1985, following important political changes in Beijing, that some of the ancient festivities were once again permitted on a regular basis. The Losar (New Year) is the most important day in the Tibetan calendar and generally falls in February. Houses are cleaned thoroughly as all dirt and anything pertaining to negativity must be ushered out with the year that is ending, and the new year greeted with a spotless environment. During the days leading up to the celebration, women prepare dozens of the most extravagantly shaped and sized fritters and place them on domestic altars, some of which are literally submerged. The fritters are offered to guests who look in on the first of the year, as it is traditional on Losar to go into the streets of Lhasa (as in other towns and villages) and see whom you can meet. The day is a continuous stream of relatives and friends.

116 top left Shortly after Losar, Lhasa celebrates Mönlam Chenmo (the festival of the Great Prayer), which is a tradition many centuries old.

116 center left The Mönlam is famous for the large quantity of statues made from torma (yak butter) that are prepared in the temples and private houses.

116 bottom left During the Mönlam, torma several yards tall used to be exhibited before 1959. Now their sizes are more modest.

116 right Everyone gets involved in the traditional celebrations for the new year and even the elderly go to pray in the temples.

Also in the first lunar month of the year, the festival of the Great Prayer, Mönlam Chenmo, is celebrated. Instituted in 1409 by the great spiritual master Lama Tzong Khapa, until 1959 the Great Prayer officially lasted for the first 15 days of the year, but, with certain additions, extended until the end of the month. During all this period, normal life in Lhasa came to a halt. In the courtyard of the east wing of the Potala, a ritual dance evoked the help of the gods to defeat evil and purify the year that was just beginning. On the third day, an endless procession of monks from Sera, Drepung, and Ganden monasteries reached the city. The abbots of the three monasteries entered the Jokhang and the civil authorities handed them the keys to the city of Lhasa. This gesture symbolized the primacy of the religious dimension over the materialness of human existence. Today much of the magnificence of the Mönlam has disappeared but it remains an important festival to Tibetans, who gather in crowds to admire the immense multicolored butter sculptures that are created on the fifteenth day in front of the Jokhang. In addition, thousands of inhabitants of Lhasa, mingled with pilgrims from across the country, form the long procession that winds through the old section of the city, preceded by a large image of Maitreya, the Buddha of the Future. The monks play their traditional instruments while the people recite the rosary, chant, and turn the prayer-wheels and the smoke of the incense spreads through the air. It is a moving sight to witness the spirituality of the Tibetan people, and only the presence of the uniforms and weapons of the Chinese soldiers who watch over the celebration prevent the visitor from thinking that time has been reversed.

117 During Losar, it is customary to visit temples and pay homage to all the altars, from those on the ground floor to the sumptuously adorned ones on the roofs.

118 top left The Shöton (the Yoghurt Festival) is one of the main celebrations in Lhasa. It begins at dawn in Drepung Monastery.

118 top right During the Shöton , a long procession of monks issues from the monastery, chanting to the sound of the instruments.

shipers with all its spiritual power. From the first to the fourth day of the seventh month, a large white tent with traditional blue decorations is raised in the large courtyard of Norbulingka. Below it, various drama companies, many of which are amateur, take turns performing some of the most popular shows of Lhamo, the peculiar form of Tibetan theater that is exclusively recreational in purpose even if the themes it deals with are religious or mythical. It is generally called "operatic" in the sense that more is sung and

118-119 To celebrate the Shöton , an enormous tanka *is exhibited on the hill just outside Drepung.*

119 top Many monks are required to unroll the protective fabric that covers the tanka*.*

119 center During the Shöton , the monks wear their characteristic yellow hat reserved for the most important ceremonies.

Another large festival held in Lhasa is the Shöton, the Yoghurt Festival, which takes place at the start of the seventh month. The name comes from what could be called the background to the Shöton: occurring in the sixth month, it falls at the end of the monastic summer seclusion when the monks are obliged to retire for a number of days and adhere to a vegetarian diet based on yoghurt. The Shöton is fundamentally a secular festival that centers on a series of theatrical performances held inside Norbulingka Palace, but it begins with a solemn religious ceremony attended by thousands of people. On the morning of the last day of the sixth month, an enormous *tanka* of the Buddha Sakyamani is displayed for several hours outside Drepung Monastery. In a clamor of noise, prayers, chants, and dance, the gigantic painting is unrolled so that it can bless the assembled wor-

120 top left The enormous painting of the Buddha Sakyamuni is revealed and is now able to bless the assembly of worshipers with its power.

120 center left The monks participating in the ceremony ensure that the painting is unrolled correctly.

120 bottom left The monks place the many silk scarves brought by the faithful as homage at the base of the immense painting.

120 right In addition to the central image of the Buddha, other figures from the Buddhist pantheon are depicted on the tanka.

120-121 The devotion of the worshipers is very powerful. In their eyes, the painted images represent the actual presence of the sacred.

danced than recited. Thousands of people of all ages sit on the ground to watch the performances that continue from morning until dusk. As Tibetan theater is a form of art based on popular culture, many of the spectators are able to understand the strengths and failings of the various performing companies, yet all are rewarded with noisy applause regardless of quality. During the four days of the festival, the courtyard of the Norbulingka is filled with songs, music, recitation, and dance, and the "marvelous stories" of the Lhamo speak with power to the hearts of the audience.

The enthusiasm with which the Tibetans still participate in the Shotön reveals an important truth: the men and women of Tibet continue to hope that their civilization is not destined to disappear and that the dramatic period that has affected the ancient and noble culture of the country for more than 40 years will one day come to an end.

126 top The festival of the Saka Dawa in the Jokhang commemorates the birth, enlightenment, and attainment of nirvana of the Buddha Sakyamuni. Rituals in Tibet are generally very long, lasting several hours. During the intervals, the monks are served traditional tea salted with yak butter.

126 bottom Personal meditation is alternated with collective prayer during ritual ceremonies.

126-127 During the rituals of the Saka Dawa, the monks wear this particular head-covering that symbolizes the five main aspects of the enlightened mind.

127 top The monks' ceremonial costume includes a special multicolored silk brocade cloak.

128 top left Roughly 35 percent of the Tibetan people are either nomadic or semi-nomadic, moving their herds between grazing lands during the various seasons.

128 top right Often nomadic women wear extremely elaborate clothes and jewelry as everyday wear.

128-129 This procession in honor of the Buddha Maitreya is held in a monastery in the region of Amdo.

129 top Although women mostly wear traditional dress, young girls are sometimes tempted by exotic "fashions."

129 bottom left The nomads in the Ngolok tribe are famous for the beauty of their traditional dress.

129 center right Despite the hard conditions of life, Tibetans almost always maintain the cheerfulness for which they are famous throughout Asia.

130-131 Even today, horses are one of the preferred means of transport and riding competitions are not uncommon at festivals.

131 top One of the proudest and most beautiful peoples in Tibet is the Khampa, who live in the region of Kham. They can be recognized by the threads of red cotton and silk that they plait into their hair.

131 bottom Nomads like this man from Xiahe in Amdo have to face the rigors of winter and therefore often wear fur hats and clothes.

132-133 Khampa women wear multicolored clothes and have elaborate hairstyles for the spectacular Litang festival, which features indigenous groups from the mountain region of Kham.

INDEX

136 Large brass cylinders, decorated on the outside with religious motifs, are typical of Tibetan art. They contain slips of paper bearing prayers and mantras. It is commonly believed that by spinning these prayer wheels on their central pin, the worshiper multiplies and diffuses the power of the prayers inside.